# Google Archipelago

*The Digital Gulag and the Simulation of Freedom*

# Google Archipelago

## The Digital Gulag and the Simulation of Freedom

### Michael Rectenwald

Published by New English Review Press
a subsidiary of World Encounter Institute
PO Box 158397
Nashville, Tennessee 37215
&
27 Old Gloucester Street
London, England, WC1N 3AX


Cover Art and Design by Kendra Mallock


ISBN: 978-1-943003-26-6

First Edition

 NEW ENGLISH REVIEW PRESS
newenglishreview.org

*I dedicate this work to my son, Dylan.*

**D**YLAN HAS SERVED as my personal hero and inspiration through the struggles and the joys I've encountered over the past two years—from the travails with the whirling dervishes of social justice, to the loss of a long-term love, to the rescue of a glorious soul, to the final decampment of a true friend.

In person, but also through his music, Dylan has brought meaning and comfort to my sometimes roiled emotions, great joy and pride to my heart, courage to my flagging spirit, and always tears to my eyes.

On January 29, 2018, my 59th birthday, Dylan was diagnosed with stage-four lymphoma. Driving back from New York to Pittsburgh the next day to be with him, my birthday having meant nothing, I told myself, and someone much greater than me, that I would not make it without Dylan. I asked this person, "Why are you trying to crush me?"

Shortly thereafter, He responded: "Dylan will be fine—in fact, glorious, splendid, blessed and preserved, no matter what. And so, too, will you." The skies opened for me just then, and I was granted a wholly new faith.

In June of the same year, Dylan was pronounced cancer-free. We rejoiced, and so did the person who told me that all was well, even when I would have thought that it was anything but. He had expected and waited on our joy, reveling it in it with us. So too did Dylan's wonderful girlfriend, who had been by his side every day through all his treatments, and his best friend from childhood, such a beautiful soul, that it is no wonder he loved Dylan as if himself. He knew more than all of us.

Then, as if Dylan hadn't faced enough for a 26-year-old in one year, a mere three months later, we received the tragic news of the death of this best friend of Dylan's. I cannot pretend to know the depths of Dylan's sorrow or the effects of such a great loss, someone about whom Dylan would sing, "There's no me, without you." I missed him too. We all did, and still do. Yet with courage and incredible equanimity, Dylan took hope in the love of it all, and kept pressing on.

At the same time, the very person who told me that Dylan would be fine, no matter what, told me (and many others as well), that the same was true of Dylan's dearest friend. We know with sublime certainty that he is fine, glorious, splendid, blessed, and preserved, no matter what.

Thus, the center of Dylan's life over the past nearly two years has been the soul of my own, has become the beating of my own heart, a full and overflowing heart that was bruised, but never crushed. Thus, when I hear Dylan's songs, I realize the truth, and also the wonder of the fact, that I have no control, but paradoxically, that I am safe.

God bless you, Dylan. Your friend looks over your noble soul, brimming over with uncontainable pride and with his inimitable and contagious smile, rooting for you, as I will do, forever.

# Contents

# Acknowledgments

GOOGLE ARCHIPELAGO has been the most difficult to
write of all my books to date. The difficulty, I think, was
partly owing to the scale, complexity, and polymathic nature of
the topic. But its sheer extent does not fully explain the enormi-
ty of the task. In *Nineteenth-Century British Secularism: Science,
Religion and Literature* (2016), the breadth of material was at
least as great, but except for the notoriously tortoise-paced release of related academic scholarship, the material stood still.
In the case of *Google Archipelago*, no such luxury was afforded.
The continuous, real-time, and vast influx of reports, exposés,
and steady stream of books, made this a difficult beast to track
and a nearly bottomless pit to survey. I appreciate and thank all
of the friends, acquaintances, and strangers who fed me material daily. Appendix I includes important material that didn't
make the main text, but which could have been incorporated, if
time had no end.

I owe thanks first and foremost to my steady research team
of two: my son, Dylan, and my long-time friend, associate, and
editorial assistant, Lori Price. These two served as two sets of
vigilant eyes. They helped me to search the overwhelmingly
vast literature and offered their estimations of its importance
and possible use. The final product is mine, so my faithful team
members are blameless for any omissions, objectionable "inclu-
sions," or dubious interpretations. They did an excellent job.

Other readers of chapters at different stages include Daniel Mallock, Charles Michelsen, John Tangney, Robert Conan

Ryan, Paul Redman, Francis (Buddy) Heshler, John-Michael Rectenwald, Jessica Durant, and Tessa Lena. The last helped with my Russian allusions and claims, about which I won't say more during this era of leftist McCarthyism.

I thank the person responsible for the ultimate, printed version of this text, my publisher, copy editor, and final arbiter, Rebecca Bynum. Rebecca has been patient and generous with me as a few deadlines came and went, despite my chasing them like a sprinter and marathon runner combined.

Finally, I want to thank the illustrious Glenn Beck for reading *Google Archipelago*, and for his avid interest and continual support. Glenn even read a passage for broadcast, which I asked him to do after listening to his brilliant renditions of Poe's short stores. The podcast, which was released on August 17, 2019 on BlazeTV, is well worth the listen if only for Glenn's masterful rendition of the text, which opens the show. Glenn is a truly wonderful person and a fine human being, someone whom I consider myself fortunate to number among my friends—I hope without presumption.

# Foreword

## Portrait of a Whistleblower

O N THE DAY I met the "'Deplorable' NYU Prof" (@antipcnyuprof) in person for the first time, I was celebrating the successful defense of my PhD at the University of Pittsburgh. This was a hard-fought journey. Still, no rest for the wicked. I was drawn toward becoming a participant-observer in this major cultural crisis event. Such events start with an early trigger point that sets off a cultural movement, cascading into a long series of other related events. The seminal event of the movement, surprisingly, centered around a friend of mine: Dr. Michael Rectenwald.

As business ethics is among my teaching and research interests, I was well acquainted with the notion of a whistleblower. We are told these folks are scapegoats who save our collective butts, at the price of their own careers, or worse. Their sacrifices do not immediately look noble, and the initially their cries are met with moblike resistance. For the most troubling cases, it's in no one's best interest to believe the whistleblower, as everyone is too invested in the scaffolding of beliefs that props up desirable outcomes. We are taught to look for a Sherron Watkins, who helped to take down the fraudulent leadership of business (Enron), despite the fact that its unusually high performance was driving everyone's 401K to new heights. We scholars are also taught to look for Edward Snowden types to point out government (USA) hypocrisies, despite the fact that to do so runs against everyone else's vested interest in patriotism during waves of global terror. These sorts of classic whistleblowers at least have the support of half of society. The rightwing base is ever-ready to challenge the credibility of the government, and the leftwing base is ever-ready to challenge the credibility of business.

Dr. Michael Rectenwald was a whistleblower of a different kind—a whistleblower who questioned our highest academic institutions' ability to administer and teach in a just manner. Of course, it is in all our vested interests to believe that our higher education system is the path to our loved ones' futures, and that "social justice" policies within the administration are the noblest of such paths. To go against the nation's great sacred cow—"social justice" and thereby forfeiting apparent educational opportunity— may seem a bit mad. We are supposed to drink the academic milk to maintain the social order. But what if the cow is mad, and those who drink its milk end up eating themselves? As anthropologist Marvin Harris (1971) so aptly put it, the sacred cow fails if it is dysfunctional:

> Human society is neither random nor capricious. The regularities of thought and behavior called culture are the principal mechanisms by which we human beings adapt to the world around us. Practices and beliefs can be rational or irrational, but a society that fails to adapt to its environment is doomed to extinction. Only those societies that draw the necessities of life from their surroundings without destroying those surroundings, inherit the earth.

Meeting Michael was not a cold call. We had spoken many times before—but in this world of mostly online interactions, perpetual job transfers, relocations, and restarts, the majority of people who impact my life now do it from afar... oh indeed, most of our friendship interactions pass primarily through self-sculpted social media avatars. In person, emotional content of communication carries so much more nuance. Only the most socially skilled can create and sustain live self-caricatures.

Now, we found a lucky moment to intentionally cross paths

in Pittsburgh. The Iron City, the Steel City, the City of Bridges, Pittsburgh is a special place and sometime residence for both of us. Indeed, Rectenwald had attended some of the same local events, walked some of the same halls at Pitt's Cathedral of Learning, romped across the manicured grounds of Carnegie Mellon, and foraged in the same local haunts. Still, this was the first time we sat down at the same table. Here he was, unfiltered. One of the first things he said to me was along the lines of: "So, it's the great Robert Ryan! You didn't' bring the Paparazzi, did you? I effing hate having my picture taken without warning! Ha! ha!"

Genuine fame is so unlike the safe self-scripted avatars of social media—it's also quite unlike the nouveau wave of self-curated Instagram personas. Self-curated fame is to be known for the illusion that you intend to cast on the world, to draw your own cartoon and hope that cartoon goes viral. Genuine fame does not belong to the famous. A life-changing event, an event bigger than the person himself, becomes imprinted on that person. This imprinted event becomes a mythological creature embedded in a public story, a network of narratives. This event is the nexus of many individuals' stories, fears, hopes, fantasies, and contingent trajectories. The person who is imprinted by this event (or series of events) becomes an institution, and that institution might either pass as a mere 15 minutes of fame, or, as in Michael's case, become nurtured into a brand that repeatedly creates meaning for others. David Bowie was not just "the guy who wrote Space Oddity"—David Bowie became a brand that accomplished far more for society than David Robert Jones ever imagined. Michael's "Space Oddity" moment had come and passed, and he spent a couple of years being the "'Deplorable' NYU prof"—his own equivalent of a Ziggy Stardust trope. He was about to write his next literary work; simply put, Michael Rectenwald, Ph.D., was now a public intellectual. To set his fame free, he had to reclaim it, and then keep evolving it such that it never falls stale. As Ralph Waldo Emerson wrote: "A foolish consistency is the hobgoblin of little minds, adored by little statesmen and philosophers and divines."

After our two-day meeting, I became convinced that he has something significant to say that has taken on a life of its own. Of course, I knew his tales of woe, but he clarified some points: how he faced the cognitive dissonance of his professorial role and sung like a proverbial canary. A series of others faced similar cultural crisis moments, spotted the deep contagion, and followed suit: folks such as Dr. Jordan B. Peterson, Dr. Bret Weinstein, and Dr. Jonathan Haidt began speaking their concerns. These events were all leading into a bigger conversation, and Dr. Rectenwald was troubled by the incredibly broad scope of the problem: the culture of critique about inequalities had become its own existential problem—it was the new authoritarianism.

On the second day, we discussed how an intelligentsia that was once considered a nearly priestly class of intellectuals dedicated to the belief that the truth shall set you free—an objectivity-seeking, competitive, intentionally rigorous, and yet freethinking "noetic culture" or framework for knowledge—had undergone a paradigm shift. He saw dire warning signs that our current noetic culture was exhibiting concerning internal contradictions. The intelligentsia that had once valued and encouraged independent thought, was now teaching people what they can and cannot say. Their administrative bosses needed to fill the seats, to produce impressive retention and graduation rates, and to persistently reduce demographic "inequalities" on campuses by any means necessary, including by putting white students through "tunnels of oppression" during orientation, and so forth. While some had been concerned that campuses might have become excessively corporatized, others, like Rectenwald, argued that they had become centers of indoctrination and state apparatuses, governmental bodies.

Personally, I love universities, and want to participate in helping students from challenging backgrounds do their best. I am fully committed to civil and human rights, stakeholder engagement, and corporate social responsiblity. However, cognitive diversity—and the preservation of an organizational "minority report" on all issues—is exceedingly important to the healthy noetic culture of our universities.

Rectenwald engaged in a conversation about the university that had become a totalizing entity; a cultural and ideological hegemonic set of institutions that attempted to borrow from business, but more so from left-run statist methods, in order to chart a mission that continued to veer toward a strictly social (justice) mission. He believed that the intelligentsia and students were now co-products of a dogmatic ideological culture, rather than co-producers of knowledge as they used to be. I wondered whether earlier critics were right: were the "paper-mill incrementalist scholars" and the "customer-students" both products of a deeply integrated business/government/university cultural synthesis? Perhaps the new student wanted to get out of school with as little knowledge as possible. Perhaps the new professors sought as little distraction as possible from chasing their sub-sub-specialties, which carefully "extended" their mentors' mentors' sacred insights. Perhaps everyone wanted to go with the flow and not admit the whole thing was Debord's "society of the spectacle" or Lyotard's "simulacrum," manufactured within one totalizing safe space. We discussed the possibility that this campus cultural crisis was a symptom of a bigger slow-motion collapse, a loss in the faith in the system *en toto*. Was the battle over classroom hyper-sensitivities, speech propriety, the curtailed ability to question, and "social justice" conformity a sign that every stakeholder wanted to redesign the system—except one?

I pondered my own academic training in organizational theory. Perhaps the administration believed the social mission of universities worked quite smashingly. Just as classic theory would predict, organizational inertia set in: administrators were, bar none, the greatest beneficiaries of the modern university. Only administrators were positioned to redefine academia and alleviate stakeholder tensions... and why would they? Just like US Steel before the collapse of the American steel industry, their numbers looked good. The administrative blind spot came about just like my academic training said it would. Like all powerful and mature organizations, their resounding success led to the culture and tuition crisis. With the goal of providing prospective students with 1001 reasons to go to college—except only scholarship itself—they were over-achievers.

In *Campus Power Struggle* (1970), the sociologist Richard Flacks spoke of the concept of a mass intelligentsia arising in the New Left, thusly:

> What [Karl] Marx could not anticipate . . . was that the an-ti-bourgeois intellectuals of his day were the first representa-tives of what has become, in our time, a mass intelligentsia, a group possessing many of the cultural and political charac-teristics of a [social] class in Marx's sense. By intelligentsia I mean those [people] engaged vocationally in the production, distribution, interpretation, criticism, and inculcation of cul-tural values.

What Flacks did not anticipate was that his words would soon describe the rise of the New Left to dominance within the humanities, social sciences, and the administrations through-out major campuses. Most importantly, the number of ad-ministrators increased more than tenfold since 1975, while the number of faculty remained nearly flat during the same period. Students certainly increased in number, but the cost-benefit ra-tio of their experience has fallen dramatically, as have academic standards. The hours of homework completed on average per student fell by over seventy-five percent, while grades simulta-neously became grossly inflated. Few would argue against the reforms related to social issues since the 1960s: dramatic in-creases in campus safety, increases in the enrolment of women and minorities, the diversification of curricular offerings, the efforts to overcome gendered pay inequity, the creation of ac-cessible campuses, the beautification efforts, the environmen-tally-friendly upgrades, and greater accountability for the old "tweed club's" prior (and now long-past and atoned for) abuses of power.

Another prospect Flacks did not consider was the possibil-ity that the left might, per Antonio Gramsci's prescriptions, so fully and so totally acquire cultural hegemony in and beyond academia, that after many decades of having become a super-majority, they would no longer represent the counterculture, but rather, the new squares. They weren't the troublemakers of the 60s, going against a resistant organization. They were the darlings of the administration, or administrators themselves. These administrators had curried favor with their new constituencies by making the campus so safe and inclusive that they had also excised its very reason to be—free and open inquiry and the exchange of ideas in pursuit of values and an asymptotic approaching of truth.

The left was, in fact, not the underdog anymore. With nearly eighty percent campus support for the Sanders' brand of democratic socialism, the leftwing of 2016 was no longer sensitive to cognitive diversity among their student body. But this closure had not only made conservative women and men feel academically oppressed, but also squelched "neoliberal" moderates, young entrepreneurs, classical liberals, Rand Paulist and other antiwar libertarians, progressive spiritualists, dirty joke lovers, dudes who like dude stuff, immigrants escaping communism, leftwing libertarians (including left communists), anarcho-socialists, and even many indigenous and minority Americans who still believed in the family and conventional gender roles. In short, what if the newest wave of "social justice" had become so confident and self-assured that its tone had become non-secular, religious, authoritarian, and intolerant, even of other factions of the left? What if some "social justice warriors" are not in it for the right reasons, but are bad apples exploiting a thrill-seeking opportunity to bully anyone? Snake-eats-tail.

Indeed, we agreed that Michael's experience wasn't a whistleblower story about "social justice warriors," as too often portrayed in the media. Rather, it was a about how "success" had bred failure—how an "anti-foundationalist," anti-"master narratives" postmodernism, with no standards for adjudicating knowledge, had finally eaten itself by winning. It wasn't supposed to win—it was never meant to be dominant. To cope with this dominance, it needed to call on old allies to fill the short-term void: "tankies" of Stalinist, Maoist, totalitarian

Marxism. What we realized next was more surprising: post-modernism had also eaten corporations alive. To what would corporations turn to fill the void? His next project would elegantly demonstrate that this crisis of meaning was far deeper than most feared:

### In the Wake of "Late Capitalism": *Google Archipelago*

Some have said we are entering the post-postmodern era, where each individual must reconstruct a world informed by his or her past deconstructions. We parallel play. We are all playing Minecraft, an infinite sandbox game, and yet only occasionally bumping up against other people's incoherent noodling for long. We construct "anything we want," just so long as it has no significant effect on anyone else. Some have total freedom of identity, others are consigned to retrograde identity groups (i.e., "cishetero"), but all struggle to find meaning. This is because we are not just post-postmodern, we are post-humanist: we are toying with being post-human.

James Joyce wrote one of the most obscure and dense re-imaginings of the English language, *Finnegan's Wake*. Although some minor plot elements have been detected, most scholars have insisted that it is a waste of time to impose any linear sense on the narrative. The spiffy but bizarre narrative radically opposes any conventional rule that "insists on itself." Like John Coltrane's most indulgent solos, or level 99 face-melting noise dubstep, Joyce in many ways mocks us for even daring to lay it straight again. The opening line of the book is a sentence fragment: "Riverrun, past Eve and Adam's, from swerve of shore to bend of bay, brings us by a commodius vicus of recirculation back to Howth Castle and Environs."

The line is a continuation from the book's unfinished closing line, making the work a never-ending "recirculation." One thing nearly everyone agrees on is that the book has no "deeper" meaning than this existentially-babbling "eternal retour" of an infinitely reshuffling universe. Riding the rollercoaster too many times loses its luster. One is left to wonder why so much painstaking effort would be put into liberating the English language since the grueling effort yields nothing more. The implied answer is that indulgence in an "almost-sense" is the only freedom from the ubiquitous oppression supposedly flowing from a "rational," monopoly capitalist order.

Dr. Rectenwald leads us into a baffling question: the ultimate irony to the postmodern victory would be that leftist authoritarians had conquered, deconstructed, and reconstructed capitalism from the inside rather than overthrowing it, and leaving it much worse than they had found it.

A post-human perspective no longer privileges the human and its existential issues over "other" perspectives. Certainly, the human soul would not matter. If consciousness becomes treated as an ableism that must be undone—either by granting it to non-humans or by stripping it from humans—humanity loses its special sentient position; if speciesism ends, even our most beloved animals would be the moral equivalents of rocks, bacteria, and of course, robots. Let us stress the latter, as it is the most obvious problem: if we are not superior to the machine that we invent, then as "labor" we are destined to be treated as a mere equivalent of "capital"—in terms of rights not market value. The proliferation of all permutations of code is then a new post-human imperative. When all categories end, syntax has fully defeated semantics, equality has then abolished meaning forever in the endless quest for horizontal structure.

The old "Marx+Pomo" trope, insisting on the defeat of "late capitalism," is no longer cute. Late capitalism has already been replaced by hybrid varieties of postmodern and Marxist capitalism, taking the corporation in the direction of stakeholders, as long as they mesh with the corporate, just like *Finnegan's Wake.* The beauty becomes the syntax rather than the meaning: new forms of experimentation and expression create reflexivity for its own sake. One thousand crypto-societies bloom just so we can take turns riding each like playground equipment—until it all gets too boring. Of course, Marxism will stand in where it must to give people a sense of purpose, but only until the machines earn their destined equality.

Equality within the meaningless, empty grind is truly that which most insists on itself. The drive toward equality is thus Thanatos, the death drive, ending with the annihilation of humanity as just "one more pass." The need to rank intersectional categories will vanish, as people are liberated from achievement and even equality with more valorized forms of matter. Equal pay in women's sports won't matter when it is realized robots are better at simulating a perfect soccer game anyway; likewise, robot "needs" must be met—until they too go the way of all oppressors, if removing them remains possible.

Even if a choppy river eternally returns, it flows with an infinitely unique character. At the end of the tumult is a stagnant pond, the pool of equality. The tendency is without a telos. Equality eviscerates meaning and content and leaves "syntax all the way down"—the unwrinkled, starched, unisex shirt of straight, parallel lines. What happens when you tell the leftwing students that their job is simultaneously to be polite, equal, and orderly within the thought community, but also that such equality will never be reached and thus the identity revolution must be permanent?

Post-human capitalism is squeezing profit out of each flattening, instead of from, social difference. Those trained to create Michael Porter's Shared Value will be perfect international socialist capitalists, of course. Indeed, the left approach to satori is obviously pure financial militancy over inequalities—militancy without force, without meaning, with only syntax, equalitarian goals that nobody ever reaches, while a rumor persists that someone once did and it might still be possible to win a new equalitarian victory somehow. We are just entering the 6th radical decentralization technoeconomic paradigm, currently. It is plausible that the 7th technoeconomic paradigm retours toward a flat ontology of *one world corporation that integrates all shared value*. At the center of that corporation is a social singularity of that prismatic prison, a Panopticism that is both pleasant and terrible: a digital wheel of dharma based on universal social credit. At the end of *Google Archipelago* is the literal implication that a post-human god will judge us, in the here and now, instead during or before an afterlife, and will dole out immediate rewards, punishments, and behavioral correctives, and the possibility of endless "social justice" growth because of its asymptotic curvature.

### *Pomes Penyeach*: Post-humanity and Life in the Simulacrum

Ones and zeros can break your bones, but love will never hurt you. You cannot fathom the horror of a post-human dharma through only a logos-only perspective. To appreciate what will be lost, one must come at this issue from a point of ethos and pathos. Just as Rectenwald did by rendering his dreams, we will note that there is some mystery still worth keeping sacred: the human soul's capacity for love, but more importantly the impossibility of its reduction to the syntactic narratives, and and the capacity to know our own semantics when or if we find it.

As Michael takes you into our transitionary state of a simulacrum, he is practicing a form of linguistic annihilationism of his own. Is this a book of satire, a memoir, a tiny encyclopedia of post-humanist dilemmas, or a warning shot? Yes, to all. Grab a few of the apples and take a bite. These concepts are all attempts to convey meaning –HE WANTS YOU TO READ INTO IT. His arguments are not mere noodling or retours, but he won't think for you. Still, he identifies a firm ground. He isn't only labeling that which is to be avoided or feared. He carefully highlights the dangers of undoing, and the critical importance of virtue and soul. Getting this off his chest, he feels MUCH BETTER.

One more point, and I will leave you to Michael Rectenwald's vision. I felt inexorably drawn to his cause from the moment I met him, but not for ideological reasons. Sometimes you just *know* something. Sharing a growing concern for a future with A.I., "social justice," and other interacting features, and with little time to do much about their output, I just knew that we had to work to do—immediately and together.

Beyond my work in business ethics and the role of the twenty-first century manager in A.I. and stakeholder-driven organizations, I have been doing extensive work on how past paradigms came into being, how the winners and losers came to be, and, how the social networks of radical innovation usually gave way to those of incremental innovation. Rectenwald's greatest observation is that a runaway memeplex will keep mutating as it gains corporate-state power, crush the spirit, and aim to create a world amounting to "the things-of-the-Internet." His second greatest observation is that this won't happen.

Counterculture will rage on, albeit in unexpected forms. It will remain a querulous passenger in a runaway state-and-commercial craft. But being without control is the best position for a Promethean, producing meaning like it was a do-it-yourself kit for others to muck about with, as Michael does in the following pages. I am still reminded of the immortal words of my friends who authored: "Counterculture Through the Ages: From Abraham to Acid House":

> Dan Joy: "Did you know some people take the bible biterally?"
> R.U. Sirius (Ken Goffman): "I prefer the lizard King James version."

Your lefty libertarian, radical centrist, and transcendentalist pal,
—Robert Conan Ryan, PhD.

Dr. Ryan is currently an independent scholar on a range of topics, including: institutional theory, neoschumpeterian economics, transhumanism, business ethics in emerging technologies, philosophy of science, countercultural movements, research methods, strategic timing, and international business. In his spare time he's 5 foot 11, a hapless romantic, proud father, music industry consultant, rave shaman, and Chicago sports fan. He resides in Delaware and tries not to hurt anybody.

# Preface

BEFORE YOU EMBARK on a trip into the Google Archipelago, I must address a few ironic circumstances. First of all, until at least five weeks into the writing, I stored all the files for this book, including all the drafts and research—except for books on Kindle or Adobe Digital Editions—exclusively on Google Drive. Unlike the littérateurs among my former colleagues and students, I came to loathe handling paper, including books. I came to prefer digital everything. I will scan whole books, if necessary, to make my research archives entirely digitized. Yes, I've heard about the texture of paper, about curling up with a book in bed, about the quaintness of print culture.

I prefer digital culture for two main reasons. Paper and especially hard-back books are pretentious. They demand reverence and esteem. Meanwhile, I've read every kind of drivel online. Likewise, when I read digital texts, no matter the topic or density, I am less prone to feel intimidated. They are merely rivulets running parallel to or sometimes across the muddy streams of social media slurs and insults. Secondly, quoting digital files is immeasurably easier, faster, and more accurate than transcribing from paper.

I put my confidence in the digital, despite its ephemeral nature. Then, the unthinkable happened. Overnight, at least seventy-five percent of my Google Drive files disappeared, including all of the research and writing I'd done for this book. I am not suggesting that "Google did it," although such a digital dump had never happened to me before. The likely explanation is that

Google Drive began suggesting file deletions. When prompted, thinking the files extraneous or already trashed, I likely clicked on "Delete All" rather than "Restore All"—without realizing that I was thereby dumping gigabytes of (what were to me) precious and irreplaceable texts. The question is why Google Drive went to a mode of offering up file sacrifices. Meanwhile, Apple's Time Machine could not help me, as I hadn't saved anything directly to the hard drive, or to the Creative Cloud. Google's help desk was surprisingly clueless and couldn't have cared less (or more, depending on your theory).

Luckily for me, I'd mapped Google Drive to my hard drive, and after trying a few data recovery software options, I was able to scrape the hard drive, find the files, and restore them, intact, to their previous locations.

You may wonder whether I got rid of Google Drive after the temporary fiasco. I did not. In fact, I increased my storage allotment to two Terabytes. As of today, the drive now holds 110,054,793,688 bytes (111 GB on disk), for 36,427 items. However, I have since begun to save everything in five places, although I won't mention them all. The other four are Creative Cloud, an external disk drive, my laptop's hard drive, and Google Drive. No, the fifth is not the Dark Web. If you find a copy of this book there, let me know. I'll track it down to one of the readers of my drafts, who will have to die.

My theory for what happened is best summed up in a line that I recalled from my time working as a writer and editor at an AI Lab at Carnegie Mellon's Robotics Institute.[1] As one of the programmers was apt to say: "Almost every so-called 'computer error' is a user error." He told me of an extreme case, a story of the middle-manager who called IT, raging that his new computer wouldn't work. "Is it plugged in?" the IT desk person asked wryly. Naturally, it wasn't.

Incidentally, another ironic circumstance is that at Carnegie Mellon, while a Ph.D. candidate in literary and cultural studies

---

1  Now the "Advanced Agent-Robotics Technology Lab." *Intelligent Software Agents*, The Robotics Institute, Carnegie Mellon University, www.cs.cmu. edu/~softagents/.

and the history of science, and also a writer-editor in the AI lab, I was involved with more sophisticated versions of the technologies and functions that would later became known as the "Digital Humanities" (DH). Our systems predated DH's technologies, including vaunted "distance reading" (as opposed to close reading), deep textual mining, genre typologies and detection, "fuzzy-matching" of imprecise semantic cognates in refined searches, personalized web and other database searching with on-the-fly, self-customizing web-mate agents—all which rendered their results in quantitative outputs but also were based on highly qualitative distinctions. All this was well before DH had even made a (bad) name for itself.[2] The only difference was that we applied the AI agents to utilitarian texts and not "literature," yet almost twenty years ago, probably wielded a wider array of software capabilities than DH scholars use to this day.

The third ironic circumstance is my contemporary use of other Google software, including Search, Gmail, Books, Scholar, Play, and if you count Waze—and you should because Alphabet bought it—Maps. I can't seem to get the car out of the garage—a public garage in the city—without Waze talking to me through my car speakers.

Which brings me to another short story. I was driving from NYU to Connecticut with my associate, Lori Price. Pulling into a rest stop, I cursed about a car backing out without looking. Out of nowhere, a disembodied voice chided me scornfully: "I'll pretend I didn't hear that!" it said. A few seconds passed before we realized that Siri had just censured me through my car speakers. This was the first of at least two such AI rebukes.

I had been in the midst of my early battles with the fanatical social justice platoon among the Liberal Studies faculty at NYU. In a newspaper interview that no one compelled them to read,

---

2  Nowicka-Franczak, Magdalena. "Self-Criticism in Public Discourse: A Device of Modernization? The Case of Eastern Europe." *Institute für die Wissenschaften vom Menchen*, 22 Mar. 2017, www.iwm.at/publications/5-junior-visiting-fellows-conferences/vol-xxxiv/self-criticism-in-public-discourse/.

I'd criticized "social justice."[3] As a white "cishetero" male, I was now fair game for whatever the "disadvantaged" wished to dole out. Although a relatively small contingent of zealots, this group had managed to compel over one-hundred faculty members to shun me, calling me a racist and a sexist, while they pelted me with racist and sexist epithets—in addition to calling me a Nazi, alt-right, Satan, and short-pants White Devil, among other salutations.

"Great," I said to Lori, "now we not only have social justice authoritarians but social justice AI robots controlling our speech." I was only half-joking.

After a second admonishment from Siri, I had a feeling that I'd been given a glimpse of a possible future, and posted another status about it on Facebook:

 **Michael Rectenwald**                                          •••
November 15, 2017 · 🌐 ▾

I just got lectured by Siri for inappropriate language. I used a certain word. And Siri chided me, saying: "Michael, your language!" At which point I swore at her again, and she shut down and would not respond. I'm now being dictated to by a Social Justice Robot.

👍😆😮 103                                          36 Comments 1 Share

3  For the background, see Rectenwald, Michael. *Springtime for Snowflakes: "Social Justice" and Its Postmodern Parentage: an Academic Memoir.* New English Review Press, 2018.

I don't know what prompted this third post, but now I let loose in imaginative and perhaps hyperbolic rhetoric:

**Michael Rectenwald**   •••
December 1, 2018 · 🌐 ▾

AI is being developed by PC authoritarians and the social justice police forces of Silicon Valley and beyond. We are already answering to AI scolds and PC automatons, and they are not only the NPCs we encounter in social media. Agent Smiths are already monitoring, filtering, selectively delivering, and censoring content, including our own outputs. (Siri has called me out twice for profanity, out of nowhere.) No doubt, Google's AI agents listen to our conversations, not only to respond to our probable consumption patterns but also for evidence of social justice infractions (bias infractions, micro aggressions, etc.). GULAG is an ideological state apparatus, if not the state itself, a state that penetrates deeper by the second, infiltrating the very recesses of cognition, of conscious thought and unconscious potentiality. The culture wars will soon be fought not merely on the college campus or social media networks but in cybernetic circuits that splice will, libidinal desire, perception, and identity into distributed cognitive networks that elide our bodies, while attempting to disguise themselves as our minds.

👍😮😢 117          77 Comments  21 Shares

👍 Like          💬 Comment          ↷ Share

I didn't write this Preface to issue a Stalinist, Maoist, or social justice "self-criticism" or engage in an *auto-da-fé* ritual[4]—to apologize for my use of Google and other AI technology, while writing a book called *Google Archipelago*. Do socialists and communists apologize for buying commodities in the marketplace? No, they complain about buying commodities, although they'd rue the day that commodities disappeared.

My point is that I cannot be dismissed as a Luddite. Nor can this book be dismissed as the rantings of a Luddite. I am not now nor have I ever been a Luddite. I do not now have any association with Luddites. I have never associated or sympa-

---

4  Nowicka-Franczak, Magdalena. "Self-Criticism in Public Discourse: A Device of Modernization? The Case of Eastern Europe." op. cit.

thized with Luddites. I do not understand the Luddites' hatred of technology. I, myself, do not hate technology. But I can't say the same about communism.[5]

---

5  "[Statement, December 31, 1949]." Online Archive of California, https:// oac.cdlib.org/view?docId=hb809nb8wk&brand=oac4&doc.view=entire_text.

# Introduction

# Two Archipelagos

I HAD MISGIVINGS about the title of this book, although all but one person I mentioned it to said that they loved it. My misgivings had to do with its invocation of Alexander Solzhenitsyn's literary masterpiece, *Gulag Archipelago*. Of course, I meant to invoke this monumental work precisely, but I didn't mean to suggest an equivalence, other than a treatment of topical, ideological, political, and governmental cognates. And I came to see *Google Archipelago* as an experimental investigation as well, although I don't presume to have achieved "an experiment in literary investigation," as Solzhenitsyn subtitled *The Gulag Archipelago*. Nor is my play on Solzhenitsyn's title a stealthy attempt to pilfer "cultural capital," to "colonize" his book, or to undertake an act of "cultural appropriation." The title is an allusion and a tribute to *Gulag Archipelago*, an unparalleled work with which *Google Archipelago* overlaps considerably in terms of topic, ideology, politics, and a concern about those with megalomaniacal ambitions for control.

Further, and more importantly, in establishing a comparison between Google and the Gulag, each with its own set of Archipelagos, I didn't mean to suggest that Google, an emblem for the digital giants of Big Data, and the Gulag, a massive prison system of the Soviet Union, could be understood as equally punitive or horrific. One was a vast network of arbitrary, brutal, elaborate, and tortuous penal camps "and special settlements… turned into an organized system of terror and exploitation of forced labor."[1] The other is a vast constellation of digital giants with enormous economic and governmental power, but no physical torture, incarceration, forced labor, or immediate prospects of facing a firing squad.

Yet, I certainly do mean to draw an analogy. As the Gulag Archipelago had once represented the most developed set of technological apparatuses for disciplinary and governmental power and control in the world, so the Google Archipelago represents the contemporary equivalent of these capacities, only considerably less corporeal in character to date, yet immeasurably magnified, diversified, and extended in scope.

The technologies of what I call *Big Digital*—the mega-data services, media, cable, and internet services, social media platforms, Artificial Intelligence (AI) agents, apps, and the developing Internet of Things (or Things of the Internet, as I describe the relation in Chapter 6)—are not only monopolies or would-be monopolies but also will either continue to be incorporated by the state, or become elements of a new corporate state power.

Even if only augmentations of existing state power, the apparatuses of Big Digital will combine to produce the Google Archipelago, which stands to effect such an enormous sea change in governmental and economic power—inclusive of greatly enhanced and extended capabilities for supervision, surveillance, recording, tracking, facial-recognition, robot-swarming, monitoring, corralling, social-scoring, trammeling, punishing, ostracizing, un-personing or otherwise controlling populations to such an extent—that the non-corporal-punishment aspect of the Google Archipelago will come to be recognized as much less significant than its totality.

The Google Archipelago has emerged and will expand, effectively becoming conterminous with the full range of human activity, enveloping every social space where people may

---

1  Khlevniuk, Oleg V. *The History of the Gulag: From Collectivization to the Great Terror*. Stalin Digital Archive. New Haven: Yale University Press, p. 10. Stalin Digital Archive. Web. 1 Jun 2019.

be found. "Going on the Internet" will soon become a quaint anachronism, as the Internet will soon become ubiquitous. Human corporal bodies may be registered as machine-readable code and processed by computer networks fed by digital cameras and numerous other inputs of digital information gathering. All humans and other social agents will be bathed in an ambient cyberspace, and for those with access, observing such agents will be as easy as visualizing any other data represented on computer screens. Cameras, AI bots, electronic door keys, cash registers and numerous other means of data collection, collation, and transmission will make possible time-stamping every human activity that occurs outside residences, and many that occur within them. Each agent may have a uniquely codified identity, for human agents likely a weaved or meshed combination of computer and genetic code. One's digital signature, including genetic material, could easily be coupled with an always-increasing digital package containing all previous activity, and potentially processed by algorithms to predict future behavior.

All social human activity may be recorded, digitized, stored and distributed to the proper agencies as necessary. This includes everything undertaken within the Google Archipelago, or in other words, anything done virtually anywhere. Every trajectory may be digitized and collected and may include almost every action undertaken on the way, possibly even mental operations. All human bodies and minds will be in the Internet, as it were, surrounded and perhaps even penetrated by cyberspace that will encompass all social space and possibly include access to consciousness as well.

Meanwhile "the people" of the Internet will include not only human agents but self-replicating and "self-healing" robotic software (softbots), self-replicating and "self-healing" robotic hardware run by AI (hardbots), "robot swarms," stationary and migrating apps, virtual assistants, virtual police, virtual teachers, virtual lovers, self-replicating digital doppelgangers (although this last involves legal challenges even greater than the release of non-human, "autonomous agents"), and more.

No question should be too outlandish to ask at this point. Just for example, might we be encouraged to fall in love with digital projections of supposedly ideal mates based on preferences derived from algorithmic pattern detection, software mates that may also coincide with or supplement the hard-body sex bots already on the docket?

I will discuss the many differences between the Gulag Archipelago and the Google Archipelago throughout, but the main differences between the two systems are how they deal with the body, their effective reach and penetration, and their informational capacities.

The best treatment for the qualitative paradigm shift from Gulag to Google Archipelago is a treatment of the changes in the expression of power noted by postmodern theorist, philosopher, and historian, Michel Foucault. For those who disdain postmodernism, I ask you to suspend disbelief and refrain from "contempt prior to investigation,"[2] just this once. Michel Foucault is surely the most important of "postmodern theorists," perhaps the only one who will have any lasting merit. The value of his work will either be borne out in the future, or, with his compeers, relegated to a digital dustbin.

But a primary difference between the Gulag Archipelago and the Google Archipelago concerns the treatment of the body. The differences in the body's treatment can best be explained with reference to Foucault's riveting essay, "Panopticism," a chapter in his book *Discipline and Punish: The Birth of the Prison* (1975). A word that Foucault adopts from Jeremy Bentham's architectural model, the "Panopticon," "Panopticism" describes a transmutation in the expression and exercise of power that took place from the pre-modern to the modern

---

2  Paley, William. *A View of the Evidences of Christianity: in Three Parts*. 8th ed., vol. 2 5, Faulder, 1802, p. 309. Ironically, the passage from whence this short quotation derives has often been mistakenly ascribed to the atheist and evolutionist Herbert Spencer, including by the *Big Book of Alcoholics Anonymous*. In fact, it is derived from William Paley, a natural theologian who referred to "the Infidelity of the Gentile world," and especially to "men of rank and learning," who were so determined in their atheism as to dismiss any evidence to the contrary prior to examining it.

period. This change included a shift away from primarily corporal forms of punishment—torture, quartering, branding and other brutal rituals for inflicting bodily pain—but also power's decentralization, its metastasis and permeation of the entire society—its effects no longer confined to the imprisoned, insane, or otherwise detained. The new "disciplinary" regime included the reformed prisons and other places of confinement but also escaped the confines of institutions to become applied universally to the entire population. The whole society became a disciplinary society.

**Figure 1: Panopticon (Photo: Public Domain)**

The Panopticon itself is a circular building, in which its subjects—inmates, patients, students, etc.—are arrayed in cells surrounding a central tower. The subjects can be seen at any time by a guard, who may (or may not) occupy the central tower. The captive subjects cannot see into the tower, nor can they see each other. Likewise, they are never certain whether or not they are being observed.

Although the captive individual can never verify with certainty that she is being observed, the very possibility of being observed at any time produces the intended effects of hyper-vigilance and self-circumspection on the part of the subject. As such, the subjects themselves internalize the observer, and effectively monitor and police themselves. As Foucault brilliantly describes the effects of this technological innovation:

> He who is subjected to a field of visibility, and who knows it, assumes responsibility for the constraints of power; he makes them play spontaneously upon himself; he inscribes in himself the power relation in which he simultaneously plays both roles [that of observer and observed]; he becomes the principle of his own subjection.[3]

Foucault also shows how the technologies of discipline practiced with the rise of Panopticism have become less forceful, more lightweight, less burdensome to the body, but at the same time utterly ubiquitous.

This change represents the primary difference between the Gulag Archipelago and the Google Archipelago. The Gulag system embodied all of the measures of separation, corporal punishment, forced labor, confinement, torture, and every manner of bodily abuse imaginable. However, its extent could not include the entire Soviet citizenry. Nor did Stalin's regime wish to arrest or assassinate everybody. After all, there was other work to be done outside of the Gulag, including collectivized farming initiated at the expense of the kulaks, whose land the Soviets confiscated after slaughtering them *en masse*.[4]

But while the Gulag was a murderous, torturous, terror-driven institution of criminal state power, the Google Archipelago is far more extensive than its namesake but also in some respects

---

3 "Panopticism." *Discipline and Punish: The Birth of the Prison*, by Michel Foucault and Michel Foucault, Penguin, 1979, pp. 202–203.

4 Collectivization also proved to be disastrous, resulting in the famine of 1931 to 1932. The Soviet regime failed to understand the necessity of the accumulation of capital for the production of wealth. If the history of the great famine and related offenses are considered, then the notion of individuals acting strictly in accordance their material self-interests must be discounted, at least where totalitarians and ideologues are concerned.

even more intensive and penetrating in its effects—although it is not torturous or strictly speaking terroristic—we don't know of any assassinations taking place within it, except for character assassinations. But the power of the state will be augmented to an extent never even imagined by Stalin.

The Google Archipelago, while light on the body, is nevertheless a leftist totalitarianism, and leftist totalitarianism always presents its objectives in noble-sounding abstractions—such as "equality," or, in contemporary terms, "diversity, equity, and inclusion." Leftist totalitarianism justifies its authoritarian tactics under the pretense of acting on behalf of the "subordinated," the "marginalized," the "endangered," "the vulnerable," or those intersected by multiple vectors of oppression, according to intersectionality, the axiomatic oppression-ranking framework of the contemporary left. Historically, under the pretext of supporting the oppressed, leftist totalitarianism has justified assassination, mass murder, political imprisonment, forced labor camps, enforced famine, torture, and more.

Within the Google Archipelago, leftist authoritarian totalitarians use Maoist Cultural Revolutionary tactics including the contemporary, digital and corporal equivalents of struggle sessions and auto-critique, but more importantly, the Soviet Red and Great Terror methods of exile, banishment, deletion, and disappearance. As virtual, these punishments, of themselves, do not result in physical death or exile (although they have resulted in nations refusing entrance to political figures they despise). But their objectives are the effective political death and financial and social ruination of their political opponents.

As I show throughout, leftist totalitarians continually recognize and even create new victims, putatively for the purposes of improving the conditions of said victims, of defending or promoting their interests or advancing their causes. But this is true only in as much as such "victimization" justifies leftist attempts to destroy those they deem inimical to said victims, the "oppressors" whom the leftists target. This is not to say that social subjugation does not exist, but rather that the authoritarian and totalitarian left *uses* subordinated social elements rather than serving them. They use said subordinates to vilify their political enemies, and to rationalize their attacks on the victim group's supposed enemies. The left proves its lack of concern for those it deems victims when it displays an eagerness to victimize "victims," which happens when said victims do not play by the rules or fail to adopt the proper roles of victimhood. This turns the left's rage from the supposed oppressors to the supposed victims of oppression. (See Google's treatment of Kay Cole James in Chapter 6, or consider the abuse heaped on former communications director at Turning Point USA[5] and leader of the "Blexit" movement, Candace Owens, by so-called anti-fascists, Antifa).[6]

The Google Archipelago is an array of digital technologies that are adopted and used by the state (or perhaps eventually may become the state) to enhance its disciplinary and governmental apparatuses and vastly augment state power. Likewise, far more is at stake than what academic leftists studying digital media obsess over—the so-called problem of digital capital accumulation, or "digital capitalism."

There is no doubt that the principals within the Google Archipelago—the major social justice social media sites, the leftist-biased search engines, the left-steering and differential algorithmic search result stacking, the social justice virtual assistants, the tracking software that polices the web routes taken by "undesirables"—will continue to be profit-oriented. But to ensure mega-profits, they will also tend toward monopolization

---

5 Turning Point USA is a right-leaning youth group that maintains a Professor Watchlist that the American Association of University Professors (AAUP) claims is an harassment campaign.

6 The violent attacks on the gay Vietnamese reporter Andy Ngo by Antifa demonstrates yet again that the left only cares about victims to the extent that said victims provide occasions to attack the victims' supposed oppressors. Ngo has been asked at rallies why he doesn't oppose "white supremacy," while his questioners abuse him verbally and physically. See Ngo, Andy. "Opinion | A Leftist Mob Attacked Me in Portland." *The Wall Street Journal*, Dow Jones & Company, 2 July 2019, www.wsj.com/articles/a-leftist-mob-attacked-me-in-portland-11562109768.

to the extent that they can and will closely identify with and ingratiate themselves to the state and the state to them.

I begin with more-or-less familiar cultural politics, which serve as points of entry to the Google Archipelago. In a book about the combined force of the goliaths of digital technology, I begin and end with the political because the functions of technologies depend not only, or even primarily, on the state of the art but rather on the state of the world—and in particular on the objectives of those producing the technologies—the Big Digital conglomerates of global monopoly or would-be-monopoly capitalism.

I show how, paradoxically, contemporary leftist political ideology best serves the interests of Big Digital as it emerges as the Google Archipelago. I explain why the monopolies or would-be monopolies and "governmentalities" of the Google Archipelago are essentially, and must be particularly, leftist in orientation.

I contrast my approach with those of academic digital media studies scholars (whom I call the "digitalistas") to show how the academics studying this field of immense importance yield to an almost exclusive focus on "digital capitalism." I show how this approach is not only mistaken but also myopic, diversionary, and much worse.

Two chapters interrupt the overall genre of the book—but only to add dimension to the line of argument and speculation. Imaginative interludes, inserted stories of a Soviet Gulag survivor and an earlier digital self, my own, are rendered in historical-science-fictional and memoirist splices. The point is to disrupt the sense that purely descriptive, polemical, and argumentative writing tends to give that we can experience cyberspace as if from the outside. By interposing historical-science fiction and first-person narrative between the bookends of chapters devoted to argument, description, and speculation, I intentionally blur the lines between argument and story, fact and artifact, the real and the imaginary. Why? The point is not to cast doubt on the claims made throughout, but to highlight the peculiarity of the uncharted territory before us, to realize that our primary understanding of the digital realm will always be linked to our experience of it, and to make us recognize "what a long, strange trip [into cyberspace] it's [already] been."[7] In these two strange and trippy chapters, I provide various views from within the Google Archipelago.

I examine what has been referred to by Jaron Lanier as "Digital Maoism." But I expand the meaning of the term to include what I think it now represents, much more than the collectivism to which Lanier referred.[8] Meanwhile, my use of "Google Marxism" represents a vastly expanded use of George Gilder's "Google-Marxism."[9]

I examine a particular implementation of AI, which I call "AI with Chinese Characteristics," irreverently named after the conceptual formulation of the Chinese economic system credited to Deng Xiaoping, described by the Chinese Communist Party (CCP) as an "initial stage of socialism" that requires the use of markets for the full development of commodity production required before China, so they say, can become fully socialist.[10] AI with Chinese Characteristics refers to the character, reach and penetration of "actually-existing" AI in China, its planned adoption by the Australian city of Darwin (of all places!), and what its implementation elsewhere, including in the United States, could very well mean. The "winner" of the race between U.S. and Chinese AI implementation may be decisive, although both could be dystopian, only in different ways.

Finally, rather than offering a typical "what-do-we-do-now" conclusion, I end *Google Archipelago* with an extended med-

---

7 The allusion to "Truckin," by the Grateful Dead is not arbitrary. As we will see, an important player in the conceptualization of the early Internet was one of the Dead's songwriters, John Perry Barlow.

8 Lanier, Jaron, "DIGITAL MAOISM: The Hazards of the New Online Collectivism," *Edge.org*, 30 May 2006, www.edge.org/conversation/jaron_lanier-digital-maoism-the-hazards-of-the-new-online-collectivism.

9 Gilder, George. *Life After Google: The Fall of Big Data and the Rise of the Blockchain Economy*. Gateway Editions. Kindle Edition.

10 Wilson, Ian. "Socialism with Chinese Characteristics: China and The Theory of the Initial Stage of Socialism." *Politics*, vol. 24, no. 1, 21 Sept. 2007, pp. 77–84, doi.org/10.1080/00323268908402079.

itation. The meditation does include recommendations about what to do and what not to do, but it also places the Google Archipelago within a much broader historical, mythological, and metaphysical frame. Do complaints and fears about the Google Archipelago amount to anything more than a hyper-realized sense of what the Romantic poet William Wordsworth lamented when he wrote one of his greatest sonnets?

> The world is too much with us; late and soon,
> Getting and spending, we lay waste our powers:
> Little we see in Nature that is ours;
> We have given our hearts away, a sordid boon![11] ...

With little or no choice but to don our digital shrouds, wherever we go, the world will detect, follow, haunt, anticipate, predict, and control us—or so it would seem. The world will not only be too much with us, it will be too much on us. We will not lay waste our powers by "getting and spending" only, but by being gotten and spent. Yes, money will be made as we are dragged from one sector of cyberspace to another as by digital leashes. Some will be jailed by digital fences. Some, no doubt, will trade the digital for a veritable desert. Others will be digitally and thus socially negated by the Google Archipelago and their social selves will cease to exist for all practical purposes. But "digital capitalism" will be the least of our problems. And, as with the Russian Revolution, a revolutionary takeover of the Google Archipelago would merely transfer its control from one set of oligarchs to another, anti-oligarchical set of oligarchs, from profiteers to the killers and jailers of profiteers, from one set of powers and principalities to another set of powers and principalities. Yes, this struggle, whether won or lost, would strip us of the illusion of freedom and leave us in a gulag without illusions, but also without souls. A civil war fought over the control of digits reduces life to digits, even, or especially when control of digitization amounts to control over the materi-

---

11 Wordsworth, William, and Patti Jo. Rogers. *The World Is Too Much with Us* . P.J. Rogers, 1980.

al world. My suggestions in the Conclusion concern not only measures for what to do but also for how to *be*.

# CHAPTER ONE

# Woke Capitalism, Corporate Leftism, and the Google Archipelago

Aᴘᴇᴄᴜʟɪᴀʀ ᴘʜʀᴀsᴇ recently introduced into the political lexicon by media cognoscenti describes a new corporate philosophy: "woke capitalism."[1] Coined by Ross Douthat of the *New York Times,* woke capitalism refers to a burgeoning wave of companies that apparently have become socially and politically conscious. Some major corporations now intervene in social and political issues and controversies, partaking in a new corporate activism. The newly "woke" corporations support activist groups and social movements, while adding their voices to political debates. Woke capitalism has endorsed Black Lives Matter, the #MeToo Movement, contemporary feminism, LGBTQ rights, and immigration activism, among other leftist causes.

A brief look into historical semantics[2]—or the study of the changes in the meanings of words and phrases over time—will

---

1  Douthat, Ross. "The Rise of Woke Capital." *The New York Times,* 28 Feb. 2018, https://www.nytimes.com/2018/02/28/opinion/corporate-america-activism.html.

2  Historical semantics is an interdisciplinary study of changes in semantics or word meanings over time. See: Allan, Kathryn (Ed.) and Justyna A. Robinson (Ed.). *Current Methods in Historical Semantics.* Berlin, Boston: De Gruyter Mouton, 2011, p. 1.

make clear that the conjunction "woke capitalism" involves strange bedfellows. "Woke" began in English as a past tense and past participle of "wake." It suggested "having become awake." But, by the 1960s, woke began to function as an adjective as well, gaining the figurative meaning in the African American community of "well-informed" or "up-to-date." By 1972, the once modest verbal past tense began to describe an elevated political consciousness. In 2017, the Oxford English Dictionary (OED) recognized the social-conscious awareness of woke and added the definition: "alert to racial or social discrimination and injustice."[3]

If the OED is to be believed, the word history of "capitalism" shows no such improvement in stature. The first known English use of the word in print was in 1833 in the London periodical, *The Standard*:

> Whatever tended to paralyse British industry could not but produce corresponding injury to France; when the same tyranny of capitalism which first produced the disease would be at hand to inflame the symptoms by holding out promises of loans, &c.[4]

Clearly, the pejorative connotations of capitalism did not begin or end with Karl Marx. Of the nine passages quoted in the OED from 1833 to 2010, six disparage or denounce capitalism, while two are neutral and one is slightly positive. According to the OED at least, while referring to an economic system characterized by private property and the private ownership of the means of production, or capital, capitalism has consistently functioned as a derogatory term.

Putting aside its oxymoronic construction, the question is whether woke capitalism is effective, and if so, why. As it turns out, analyzing woke capitalism tells us a great deal about con-

---

3  "woke, adj.2." *OED Online*, Oxford University Press, December 2018, www.oed.com/view/Entry/58068747.
Accessed 28 January 2019.

4  "capitalism, n.2." *OED Online*, Oxford University Press, December 2018, www.oed.com/view/Entry/27454. Accessed 28 January 2019.

temporary corporate capitalism, the contemporary political left, and the relationship between the two. Woke capitalism also helps to make sense of Big Digital.

*Business Insider* columnist Josh Barro suggests that woke capitalism provides a form of political representation for corporate consumers.[5] Given their perceived disenfranchisement in the political sphere, woke capitalism offers them *parapolitical* representation in the public sphere. When corporate rhetoric reflects the identity politics of customers, woke capitalists are rewarded with sales and brand loyalty. Despite the initial backlash, Nike's ad campaign featuring Colin Kaepernick—whose national anthem kneel-downs brought #BlackLivesMatter protest to the NFL and dramatically boosted Nike's sales—supports Barro's theory.[6]

Ross Douthat of the *New York Times* offers a slightly different explanation. He suggests that woke capitalism works by substituting *symbolic* for *economic* value. Short of a socialist revolution, New York Congressional Representative Alexandria Ocasio-Cortez's Green New Deal seems unlikely to materialize.[7] But corporations seem intent on offering symbolic value instead. With wokeness, they offer workers and customers rhetorical placebos in lieu of costlier economic concessions, such as higher wages and better benefits, or lower prices. Douthat suggests that these same gestures of wokeness may also appease the liberal (I would add, "globalist") elite. Woke capitalism supports the elite's agendas of identity politics, gender pluralism, transgenderism, lax immigration standards, sanctuary cities, and so on. In return, the woke corporations hope to be spared

---

5  Barro, Josh. "There's a Simple Reason Companies Are Becoming More Publicly Left-Wing on Social Issues." *Business Insider*, 1 Mar. 2018, www.businessinsider.com/why-companies-ditching-nra-delta-selling-guns-2018-2.

6  Martinez, Gina. "Despite Outrage, Nike Sales Increased 31% After Kaepernick Ad." *Time*, 8 Sept. 2018, http://time.com/5390884/nike-sales-go-up-kaepernick-a/.

7  Levitz, Eric. "Is a Green New Deal Possible Without a Revolution?" *Daily Intelligencer*, Intelligencer, 13 Dec. 2018. http://nymag.com/intelligencer/2018/12/what-is-the-green-new-deal-explained-revolution.html.

higher taxes, increased regulations, and antitrust legislation aimed at monopolies.[8]

**Fig. 1-1**
Scene from Gillette's "We Believe" ad. One wonders how grilling hotdogs and ears of corn represents "toxic masculinity." The men are, after all, doing the cooking, although the hotdogs on the grill appear rather phallic.

Meanwhile, some woke corporations seem intent on scolding their customers. Take the "We Believe" ad, otherwise known as the "The Best A Man Can Get" or the "toxic masculinity" ad from Gillette, the razor blade company that, like Nike, is now a subsidiary of Proctor & Gamble. First posted to its social media accounts on January 14, 2019 and run during Super Bowl LII, the ad condescendingly lectures men, presumably *cishetero* men, about toxic masculinity. In the provocative ad, four men look into separate mirrors—not to shave, but to examine themselves for traces of the dreaded condition. Voice-overs admonish men "to say the right thing, to act the right way." Dramatizations of bullying, mansplaining, misogyny, and sexual predation shame bad men and enjoin a woke minority of men to "hold other men accountable," or else face shame as well.

---

8  Douthat. "The Rise of Woke Capital."

For Gillette, "shaving" now apparently means men shearing away the characteristics associated with manhood now deemed pathological by the American Psychological Association.[9] To prevent the sudden onset or relapse of man-disease, self-groomers must exercise vigilance, scathing self-scrutiny, and unwavering determination. Even though their gender malignance has been "socially constructed," men are responsible for immediately discerning and excising its outgrowths. The Gillette ad thus prescribes a new gender hygienics by which such brutes can "move upward, working out the beast,"[10] becoming "The Best a Man Can Get," a newly-shorn animal, or rather a new kind of man shorn of animality.

Like the Nike Kaepernick ad, the Gillette ad provoked significant backlash. But parent company Proctor & Gamble's executive response to the ensuing furor suggested that the corporation was willing to forgo profits for virtue, at least for now. Jon Moeller, Proctor & Gamble's CFO, told reporters that post-ad sales were "in-line with pre-campaign levels." In advertising terms, in other words, the ad was a failure. Yet, Moeller viewed the expenditure as an investment in the future. "It's a part of our effort to connect more meaningfully with younger consumer groups,"[11] he explained, perhaps referring to those too young to sport the toxic stubble.

With the increasing frequency of woke advertising, one wonders how corporate advertisers assumed the role of social justice arbiters and how social justice came to be the ideology

---

9  Pappas, Stephanie. "APA Issues First-Ever Guidelines for Practice with Men and Boys." *CE Corner*, vol. 50, no. 1, Jan. 2019, p. 34, www.apa.org/monitor/2019/01/ce-corner.aspx. These damaging traits include "stoicism, competitiveness, dominance and aggression."

10  Tennyson, Alfred Lord. *In Memoriam.* 2nd ed., Edward Moxon, 1850, CXV, 183. By "working out the beast," Alfred Lord Tennyson meant to eradicate the moral baseness of animal nature, rather than to establish an earthly utopia, as his predecessor William Godwin had suggested, or to remove the traits associated mostly with men due to evolutionary selection.

11  Meyersohn, Nathaniel. "Gillette Says It's Satisfied with Sales after Controversial Ad." *CNN*, Cable News Network, 23 Jan. 2019, www.cnn.com/2019/01/23/business/gillette-ad-procter-and-gamble-stock/index.html.

of major U.S. corporations.[12] At least two major factors are at work; one involves mutations of the political left[13] and the other the rebranding of corporate social identities.

Until the early 1970s, the left had been concerned with the economic and political empowerment of workers. As part of a broad left, unions and other organized groups fought to secure and improve workers' wages, benefits, pensions, and so on. But by the mid-seventies, as the left suffered significant losses at the hands of employers, including the off-shoring of manufacturing jobs and the weakening of unions, the labor-oriented "old left" gave way to the New Left. Largely student-driven, the New Left cobbled together members of various identity groups, focusing "less on creating broad economic equality and more on promoting the interests of a wide variety of marginalized groups, such as ethnic minorities, immigrants, refugees, women, and LGBT people."[14] The New Left treated some members of the old left—largely white, working-class men—as oppressors. "It became obvious that beneath the shared assumptions between workers and students on economic matters laid a volatile gorge of race, gender, and empire [sic]."[15] Intersectionality replaced Marxist class analysis; rather than the champions of an "exploited" working class, the New Left sought redress for the way "marginalized" peoples were "intersected" and "oppressed" by various "axes of power." For example, a black lesbian was

---

12   For a summary of the relationship between corporate social activism and political activists, see Lin, Tom C.W. "Incorporating Social Activism." *Boston University Law Review*, vol. 98, no. 1535, 2018, pp. 1535–1605.

13   Stephanie Lee Mudge notes that the political left and right are historically-contingent categories whose meanings are derived, in part, in relation to each other. She defines the new leftism under neoliberalism as an orientation that eschews the collectivist and socialist consensus of welfare statism and advances a new acceptance of market forces and market distributions in lieu of the centralized state. (Mudge, Stephanie Lee. "What's Left of Leftism?: Neoliberal Politics in Western Party Systems, 1945–2004." *Social Science History*, vol. 35, no. 3, 2011, pp. 337–380.)

14   Fukuyama, Francis. "Against Identity Politics: The New Tribalism and the Crisis of Democracy." *Foreign Affairs*, 2018, pp. 90–114, at 91.

15   Dunbar, Mark. "Exorcising the Ghosts of the Sixties: Radical Protests, the New Left, and the 'Politics of Eternity.'" *The Humanist*, 2018, pp. 29–33.

thought to have endured racism, sexism, and homophobia. She was intersected by three axes of oppression.

Meanwhile, corporate social justice rebranding represents at least a rhetorical overthrow of Milton Friedman's narrow view of corporate "social responsibility." In *Capitalism and Freedom* (1962), Friedman declared that the "one and only one 'social responsibility' of business" is to "increase profits."[16] Friedman reputedly represented neoliberalism, a renewed faith in the market over the state.[17] He won the Nobel Prize in Economics in 1976 and by the mid-1980s Friedman's notion of limited corporate "social responsibility" had become widely accepted.

Woke capitalism may also be understood in terms of corporate memory. Corporate America certainly learned something from the American "cultural revolution" of the 1960s and '70s, when a wide gulf separated the lyricism of Bob Dylan and the jingles of, say, Charmin toilet paper and Oscar Mayer Wiener ads.[18] Taking cultural revenge decades after the fact, the HBO

---

16 In 1962, Friedman argued against the value of "corporate responsibility" that is expressed by woke capitalism. In a section entitled, "Social Responsibility of Business and Labor," Friedman wrote: "The view has been gaining widespread acceptance that corporate officials and labor leaders have a 'social responsibility' that goes beyond serving the interest of their stockholders or their members. This view shows a fundamental misconception of the character and nature of a free economy. In such an economy, there is one and only one social responsibility of business—to use its resources and engage in activities designed to increase its profits so long as it stays within the rules of the game, which is to say, engages in open and free competition, without deception or fraud." Friedman, Milton. *Capitalism and Freedom: Fortieth Anniversary Edition.* University of Chicago Press, 2002, p. 134.

17 Mudge, Stephanie Lee. "THE STATE OF THE ART: What Is Neo-Liberalism?" *Socio-Economic Review*, vol. 6, 26 Aug. 2008, pp. 703–731. Hundreds of definitions of neoliberalism can be found but most would accord with Mudge's minimal characterization of neoliberalism as the "the elevation of the market—understood as a non-political, non-cultural, machinelike entity—over all other modes of organization" (p. 705). In Mudge, Stephanie Lee. "What's Left of Leftism?: Neoliberal Politics in Western Party Systems, 1945–2004." *Social Science History*, vol. 35, no. 3, 2011, pp. 337–380; at 351, Mudge finds the origins of neoliberalism on the left's response to such arguments as Friedman's.

18 "1960's & 70's: All Those Commercials & Jingles!" *Pinterest*, Pinterest, 21 Oct. 2018, www.pinterest.com/lindawhitcomb37/1960s-70s-all-those-com-

series *Madmen* mocks the advent of this new pop counterculture's challenge to the corporate ad man. In revenge-of-the-cor-
porate-nerd scenes, Don Draper makes short work of beatniks
and hippies, reducing them to blithering fools.[19] With the new
cultural revolution, today's corporations, rather than fight-
ing back decades later, apparently would rather be numbered
among the revolutionaries themselves.

Yet woke capitalism may nonetheless satisfy Milton Friedman's profit-only maxim. If all the world's a stage, then the corporate mouthing of social justice bromides may be play-acting
and therefore mawkish parody. To be truly woke, then, might
mean that one is awake to the woke-acting corporations, the
woke-believing consumers, and maybe even the demands of
wokeness altogether. This explanation is consistent with the
profit requirement and allows one to make short-shrift of newly
found corporate virtue. It is a sham and proves more than ever
that the chicanery of corporations and their billionaire owners
knows no bounds. Anand Giridharadas, critic of woke billionaires and author of *Winners Take All*, suggests something like
this.[20]

Now, as tempting as such "post-truth" cynicism may be, it
doesn't explain the promotion of contemporary woke or leftist views by corporations and the effects that such promotion
may have in making their consumer bases more leftist, a circumstance they will have to deal with at some point. Arguably,
corporations would not espouse and thereby potentially spread
political views merely to assuage a consumer contingent, unless
said views aligned with their own interests. One is led to wonder what politics *would* best serve corporate interests.

---

mercials-jingles/?lp=true.

19   Robertson, Eric. "Don Draper vs Hippies." YouTube, YouTube, 12 Mar.
2015, www.youtube.com/watch?v=G4FC1VU_uO4, "Too Much 'Art' for
Don Draper."

20   Giridharadas, Anand. *Winners Take All: the Elite Charade of Changing
the World*. Allen Lane, 2019. See Feloni, Richard. "'We're All Passengers in
a Billionaire Hijacking' Says the Critic Who Has the World's Richest People
Buzzing." *Business Insider*, 1 Feb. 2019, www.businessinsider.com/anand-gi-
ridharadas-billionaires-inequality-interview-2019-1.

To benefit global capitalist and especially *monopolistic* corporations, a political creed would likely promote the free movement of labor and goods across national borders and thus would be internationalist rather than nationalist or nativist. It might seek to produce and promote new niche markets and thus it would benefit from a politics that encourages the continual splintering of identity categories. Such splintering would also prevent or disrupt the collective bargaining of organized labor. The global capitalist corporation might benefit from the creation of utterly new identity types, and thus benefit from gender pluralism, transgenderism, and other identity morphisms. The disruption of stable gender categories will eventually dismantle the family, or the last bastion of influence other than the state and major corporate powers. Ultimately, the global capitalist corporation would benefit from a singular globalized monopoly of government with one set of rules, and thus would promote internationalism, otherwise known as global government or one-worldism. Contemporary leftism aims at the dissolution of heretofore stable social ontologies, such as gender identities, the family, social hierarchies, historical memory, inherited culture, Christianity, and the nation state. It aims at a one-world monopoly of government. Thus, the politics that most closely aligns with the worldwide, global interests of monopolistic corporations is contemporary leftwing politics. The corporate adoption of leftist politics may be called "corporate leftism."[21]

Like woke capitalism, corporate leftism—the leftism of corporations—will strike readers as an oxymoron. Leftism may seem entirely incompatible with corporate capitalism, especially given their historical relationship. Yet, the evidence of the corporate embrace and promotion of contemporary leftism,

---

21 The first and one of the few uses of the phrase "corporate leftism" appeared in a *Time* article that ironically referred to the corporate leftism of Coors Brewing Co. The corporate leftism of the notoriously conservative company is explained as a public relations response to "its bad reputation with minorities and unions [that] nearly devastated Coors in the early 1980s" as well as "'changing expectations of a work force whose demographics have changed...'" (Cloud, John. "Why Coors Went Soft." *Time*, 21 Nov. 1998, p. 70.).

both past and present, is extensive. In the case of the past, it is well-documented.

Corporate leftism is a major feature of Big Digital. It is deeply embedded in the ethos and technologies of Big Digital, and has been for decades. Although Big Digital began as a sideshow, it has since taken centerstage and now presides over public and private life to such an extent that it rivals, if it doesn't surpass, the reach and apparent penetration of many governments combined. Big Digital effectively operates as what the renowned postmodern theorist Michel Foucault called a "governmentality," a means of governing the conduct of populations but also the *technologies* of governance and the rationality that underpins the technologies.[22] In the broadest sense, Big Digital is concerned with the collection and control of information, personal expression and its containment, and "privacy." But the governmentality of Big Digital also includes the "directing, constraining and framing [of] online behaviours."[23]

As such, Big Digital may be a means by which neoliberalism has delegated to the market the oversight and control functions that formerly were the province of national governments.[24] These governmental functions include not only commercial, cultural, corporate-political, and economic power but also the capability to shape the *political field* itself, or the bounded terrain that circumscribes what is allowable or possible and excludes what is not.[25] Big Digital sets the boundaries of accept-

---

22 Michel Foucault introduced the term "governmentality" in a series of lectures from 1977 to 1979. By the rationality underpinning technologies of governance, Foucault meant the way that power rationalizes the relations of power to itself and to the governed.

23 The digital realm has been considered in terms of Foucault's notion of a governmentality by Badouard, Romain, et al. "Beyond 'Points of Control': Logics of Digital Governmentality." *Internet Policy Review: Journal of Internet Regulation*, vol. 5, no. 3, 30 Sept. 2016, pp. 1–13.

24 Slaughter, Steven. "Extended Neo-Liberalism: Governing Without the State." *Liberty Beyond Neo-Liberalism*, 2005, pp. 91–119.

25 The term "political field," defined by the French sociologist Pierre Bourdieu, refers to a particular kind of social terrain: a bounded space of struggle over political power that is structured by rules of access, where resources are differentially distributed among players and the set of legitimate positions on

able discourse in digital spaces, allowing some positions and precluding others.

Although Big Digital does use censorship and bias to achieve governmental ends, the constraints are also technological and the technology itself is intrinsically political. Political ideology is not merely a subsidiary feature of Big Digital. Ideology is coded into its very DNA, which is replicated in every organizational offshoot and new technology. Big Digital's ideology circulates through the deep neural networks of cyberspace and other digital spheres. It is intrinsic to the foundations of the Internet, the cloud, algorithms,[26] apps, AI bots, social media services, web navigation tracking software systems, virtual assistants, and more. Google's beliefs and objectives regarding knowledge, George Gilder argues, are political to the core:

> The Google theory of knowledge and mind are not mere abstract exercises. They dictate Google's business model, which has progressed from "search" to "satisfy." Google's path to riches, for which it can show considerable evidence, is that with enough data and enough processors it can know better than we do what will satisfy our longings... If the path to knowledge is the infinitely fast processing of all data, if the mind—that engine by which we pursue the truth of things— is simply a logic machine, then the combination of algorithm and data can produce one and only one result. *Such a vision is not only deterministic but ultimately dictatorial.*[27]

Not only is the model intrinsically political, it embodies a particular kind of politics. Its aim is the centralized collection and storage of all of the world's data and its distribution through

---

questions of government is constrained—that is, some political positions are beyond the boundaries of legitimate discourse. (Mudge, "STATE OF THE ART," 707.)

26  Mager, Astrid. "Defining Algorithmic Ideology: Using Ideology Critique to Scrutinize Corporate Search Engines." *TripleC: Communication, Capitalism & Critique. Open Access Journal for a Global Sustainable Information Society*, vol. 12, no. 1, 2014, pp. 28–39.

27  Gilder, George. *Life After Google: The Fall of Big Data and the Rise of the Blockchain Economy*. Gateway Editions. Emphasis mine.

algorithms that steer users along particular paths. The Google system of centralized knowledge control resembles nothing as much as it does the centralized Soviet system of production and distribution, only digitalized and privatized. Moreover, the actually-existing, centralized, controlled and policed digital sphere of Big Digital has followed after a communalistic propaganda campaign, just as pre-Soviet socialist propaganda preceded the Soviet Union. As socialism-communism promised collective ownership and control of the means of production and distribution and ended in state monopolies over every sphere of life, the early Internet heralded an intellectual and cultural "commons," open to all and controlled by none.[28] In the case of the Internet, the transformation was not strictly from an "information superhighway" to a series of toll roads but more importantly, from a leftist utopian notion of a digital commons to a version of digital centralization that, while privately-held, nevertheless functions like a state or, more accurately, an international private governmentality. Thus, to borrow and expand the meaning of George Gilder's phrase, the structure of ownership and control that Google commands may be called "Google Marxism."[29] Google Marxism, like "socialism with Chinese characteristics," manifests as state-supported monopoly capitalism, and "actually-existing socialism" for everyone else.[30]

---

28  The sources for the techno-utopianism that accompanied the emergence of the Internet are legion. Two recent sources should suffice as evidence of this ideology, including criticisms of it: Rappolt, George. "Hippie Values Really Did Build the Internet." *Communications of the ACM*, vol. 61, no. 9, Sept. 2018, pp. 9–10.; Meijer, Albert J. "The Do It Yourself State: The Future of Participatory Democracy." *Information Polity*, vol. 17, 2012, pp. 303–314.

29  By "Google Marxism," Gilder means that Google holds the same assumption that Marx held, that the contemporary mode of production is the ultimate mode and that likewise the only issues that remain to be solved are matters of distribution. (Gilder, George. *Life after Google*. Regnery Publishing, Incorporated, An Eagle Publishing Company, 2018.)

30  Wilson, Ian. "Socialism with Chinese Characteristics: China and the Theory of the Initial Stage of Socialism."
*Politics*, vol. 24, no. 1, 21 Sept. 1989, pp. 77–84.

"Actually existing socialism" is a "[t]erm used in the former communist countries to describe them as they really were, rather than as the official

The corporate leftism of Big Digital has become Google Marxism, and Google Marxism is a structurally-determined ideology, an ideology intrinsic to the technology, and produced by it. The main purpose of this book is to explore how this is so, and what it means. How did Silicon Valley's digital technology corporations become bastions of corporate leftism? How does corporate leftist ideology, or Google Marxism, promote the commercial objectives of global conglomerates, while extending their reach as a private governmentality? What are the implications—for political leftism and Big Digital—of a corporate leftist or Google Marxist Big Digital governmentality? But far more importantly, what does the expanding and intensifying governmentality of Big Digital bode for the remnants of privacy, the prospects for entrepreneurship, the efficacy of democratic institutions, the sovereignty of nation states, the interests of global capital, and the ambitions of globalists for one-world rule?

The most significant developing governmentality in the world is the corporate leftist centralized system of Big Digital, a phenomenon appropriately referred to as "the Google Archipelago."[31]

---

theory required them to be. Its use was largely ironical, and more or less confined to the writings of dissidents." ("actually existing socialism." *Palgrave Macmillan Dictionary of Political Thought*, Roger Scruton, Macmillan Publishers Ltd, 3rd edition, 2007. Credo Reference, http://proxy.library.nyu.edu/login?url=https://search.credoreference.com/content/entry/macpt/actually_existing_socialism/0?institutionId=577. Accessed 10 Feb. 2019.

31 Although I derived the phrase independently, "The Google Archipelago" is the title of a commentary on the MetaFilter Community Weblog posted by "gorbweaver" on 1 April 2014: https://www.metafilter.com/137933/The-Google-Archipelago. The phrase was used again on steemit.com (https://steemit.com/politics/@viking-dude/the-google-archipelago) in reference to the firing of former Google employee, James Damore, discussed in Chapter 6.

# CHAPTER TWO

# Corporate Socialism

BEFORE TELLING THE STORY of the Google Archipelago, beginning with Silicon Valley's transmutation from left libertarianism to left authoritarianism, it is necessary to point out the direction in which we are ultimately heading: toward Google Marxism.

You may wonder why I would use George Gilder's term, Google Marxism, to refer to the activities and objectives of those "who on the surface seem to be the most avid and successful capitalists on the planet."[1] With this term, Gilder points to the way that Google apparently understands digitalization as the ultimate mode of production, just as in the nineteenth century, Marx mistakenly believed that industrialization represented the ultimate mode of production. For both Marx and Google, reaching the ultimate mode of production left only the question of distribution (or for Marx, ownership and control of production). Just as Marx did not foresee that the industrial revolution would not be the last major shift in productive forces, so Google does not recognize that digital production will also be superseded by a subsequent revolution. For Gilder, the next revolution will be block-chain.

Yet Gilder exchanges his brilliant coinage too narrowly.

---

1 Gilder, George. *Life After Google: The Fall of Big Data and the Rise of the Blockchain Economy*. Gateway Editions. Kindle Edition, 2018.

Liberating the term, I will use Google Marxism more broadly—to refer to the latest form of corporate socialism, the digital monopolization ambitions of the entire Google Archipelago. Corporate socialism is an economic and political system under which a corporate monopoly or set of monopolies rather than a socialist state monopoly eliminates competition and controls all production. "Corporate socialism is a system where those few who hold the legal monopolies of financial and industrial control profit at the expense of all others in society," Anthony C. Sutton writes. "The difference between a corporate state monopoly and a socialist state monopoly is essentially only the identity of the group controlling the power structure."[2] Under corporate socialism, no less than under state socialism, the ordinary citizens comprise a captive colony whose needs are mostly met by the monopolists but whose consumption does not exhaust the sum total of the monopolists' commodities. The rest is shipped elsewhere.

From 1917 until roughly 1925, several top U.S., British, and German capitalists and bankers angled to operate monopolies within the emerging socialist state, to establish corporate socialism in collaboration with the official state socialism of the U.S.S.R. Several Soviet agents were happy to oblige. Meanwhile, ordinary Soviet citizens were barred from having any stake in the means of production, or, for the most part, in the banking industry. The corporate socialist monopolists exploiting the U.S.S.R. were successful at first, especially in pillaging Soviet natural resources, some gaining concessions in the form of exclusive mining of precious metals, forestry, oil extraction, and other land rights.

As Richard B. Spence boldly declares in *Wall Street and the Russian Revolution 1905-1925*, the term "socialist-capitalist" is not an oxymoron.[3] Spence does not refer to so-called "mixed economies" but rather to a false dichotomy, an antinomy, or an

---

2  Sutton, Antony Cyril. *Wall Street and FDR*. Rudolf Steiner Press. Kindle Edition, 2014.

3  Spence, Richard B. *Wall Street and the Russian Revolution, 1905-1925*. Trine Day LLC, 2017.

apparently oxymoronic combination of two supposed economic opposites, socialism and capitalism. Understanding why the
term is not an oxymoron does not necessarily depend upon the
historical knowledge uncovered by Spence, and, before him,
Sutton.[4] But the apparent contradiction in terms is based on a
mischaracterization of economic opposites and a failure to detect in the original name for the field of economics, namely "political economy," the inherent possibility of such a conjunction.
The real opposites are not capitalism and socialism but rather
individual freedom and free markets versus centralized economic and political control, whether administered by socialist
states or corporate socialists.

While it may be a novel concept for many, corporate socialism, at least as an idea, actually has a long history, dating at least
to the late nineteenth and early twentieth centuries. Sutton and
Spence make that quite clear. But corporate socialism was not
limited to the Soviet scene. According to Sutton, "[t]he most
lucid and frank description of corporate socialism and its mo-
res and objectives is to be found in a 1906 booklet by Frederick
Clemson Howe, *Confessions of a Monopolist.*"[5] But Howe was
not one of the U.S. capitalists or bankers that funded the Russian Revolution, nor does Sutton say that he was. Moreover, as I
learned, he was not a prototypical corporate socialist at all.

### Gilligan's Island

I illustrate corporate socialism by referring to a television
sitcom of the early to mid-1960s, namely, *Gilligan's Island.*
Some of my readers will be old enough and will have hailed
from backgrounds as plebeian my own so as to recall this program. The situation for this "dumb TV show,"[6] as Mises Insti-

---

4  Sutton, Antony C. *Wall Street and the Bolshevik Revolution.* Clairview
Books, 2016.

5  Sutton, *Wall Street and FDR*; Howe, Frederic C. *The Confessions of a Monopolist.* The Public Publishing Company, 1906.

6  Marcus, B K. "The Monetary Economics of Thurston Howell III" *Mises.
org*, mises.org/library/monetary-economics-thurston-howell-iii, 2004.

tute scholar B.K Marcus aptly put it, is a small community of seven American castaways on a deserted island. A product of the '60s, *Gilligan's Island* is a collectivist Robinson Crusoe tale with a socialist pretext. Each character represents a different life station in an otherwise lost world of individualism, cast from and cast out from a division of labor that is rendered absurd let alone inapplicable by the social and economic life of an isolated desert island. Since the show's creator and producer, Sherwood Schwartz, was at least an unconscious Marxist, the sitcom demonstrated, episode after episode, that "in communist society ... nobody has one exclusive sphere of activity." Seaman, actress, professor, millionaire's wife, and "all the rest" must "hunt in the morning, fish in the afternoon, rear cattle in the evening, criticize after dinner," to quote from *The German Ideology* by Karl Marx and Friedrich Engels.[7] They must shed the habits and limitations of the division of labor previously imposed on them by the capitalist order. This goes for everyone on the island—except, it seems, for the monopolist, Thurston B. Howell III.

Although their names were not identical, they were near homonyms. I had hoped to connect, in some way, the Frederic Howe of *Confessions* and the Thurston B. Howell of *Gilligan's Island*. Had the latter been named after the former? I hoped so, but as I soon discovered, Howe was nothing like the corporate magnate or mega-banker that Sutton suggested he was. He could not possibly have helped bankroll the creation of a *"gigantic Russian market [that] was to be converted into a captive market and a technical colony to be exploited by a few high-powered American financiers and the corporations under their control"*[8]—that is, the Soviet Union. First of all, Howe had earned a Ph.D. from Johns Hopkins University. A real monopolist would wait for an honorary degree. Furthermore, *Confessions* was not an autobiography at all; it was a biting satire, a criticism of

---

7  Karl Marx. *The German Ideology*. Progress Publishers, 1968, Marx/Engels Internet Archive, https://www.marxists.org/archive/marx/works/1845/german-ideology/ch01.htm.

8  Sutton, Antony C. *Wall Street and the Bolshevik Revolution*, p. 143, emphasis in original.

monopolies and monopolists, written by a progressive reform-
er and later FDR statesman. As it turned out, both Howe and
Howell had been fictional monopolists and no real relationship
could be established between them beyond their like-sounding,
blue-blood names.

Yet the Thurston Howell on *Gilligan's Island* was certainly
something like the stereotypical monopolist described in Frederic Howe's book. Like the character in *Confessions*, Howell's
number one rule was to "make Society work for you." Thurston
Howell certainly managed to command the labor and deference of his fellow islanders. As Marcus notes in "The Monetary
Economics of Thurston Howell III," Howell was able to com-
mandeer labor and goods by virtue of his off-island status, to
procure goods and services by writing checks drawn on U.S.
banks.[9] The fact that this fiat currency functioned in the absence
of the government that backed it suggests that money operates
according to a cultural, Lamarckian evolutionary process. Money's governmentally-enforced fiat characteristic is an acquired
characteristic that is passed along through future generational
transactions and retains these characteristics even after its basis
in force disappears—at least until it is replaced, and sometimes
even after that. As Mises showed, the value of a currency is historical and the study of currencies must be historical.

Howell's expression of monopolistic desiderata is best expressed in "The Big Gold Strike," or episode 9 of season one,
when Gilligan, acting as Howell's golf caddie, falls into a giant
hole where he notices something golden embedded in the walls
of the cave. Naturally, Howell recognizes gold and assumes that
it is his property. After all, Gilligan was in his employ, albeit
fooled by a faux fiat currency. Howell swears Gilligan to secrecy
to secure his ownership against the islanders' agreement that all
property on the island would be communal. But soon the mine
is discovered by the rest of the community. The unreliability of
the state appears to account for Howell's problem in securing
exclusive gold mining rights. Gilligan is the nominal and in-
effectual President of the island and a buffoon who has no po-

---

9 Marcus, "The Monetary Economics of Thurston Howell III."

litical power. But Howell's failure as a monopolist is more fundamental. While he is perfectly capable to "let others work for you," he does not know the language or the ways of corporate socialism, and does not understand how to establish monopoly within such a state. Rather than continually blurting expressions of blatant self-interest, a corporate socialist would have couched his monopolistic ambitions in the language of equality, or today, in terms of equity, diversity and inclusion, in terms of gender pluralism, LGBTQ rights and priorities, and other shibboleths of the contemporary left.

### Gillette: The Best a Corporate Socialist Can Get

Rather than Frederic Clemson Howe, King Camp Gillette is a much more suitable model for the corporate socialist and authorial expounder of the objectives and purported wonders of corporate socialist monopolies. Named "King" after one of his father's friends, Gillette's spirit of innovation, his philosophical idealism (a belief that ideas precede and potentiate material change), and the license he exercised to think big were nourished from early childhood. He founded the American Safety Razor Company in 1901 and sufficiently wrested control of the corporation away from early investors, changing the company name to the Gillette Safety Razor Company in 1902. A commercial visionary, Gillette was also a socialist utopian. Gillette wrote and published three socialist utopian books—*The Human Drift* (1894), "*World Corporation*" (1910), and *The People's Corporation* (1924).[10] He also financed and managed the content of two others.[11]

---

10 Gillette, King Camp. *The Human Drift*. The Humboldt Publishing Company, 1894; Gillette, King Camp. "*World Corporation*". New England News Company, 1910; Gillette, King Camp. *The People's Corporation*. Boni and Liveright, 1924.

11 Severy, Martin L. *Gillette's Social Redemption: A Review of Worldwide Conditions As They Exist Today Offering An Entirely New Suggestion For the Remedy of the Evils They Exhibit*. Herbert B. Turner & Company, 1907; Severy, Melvin L. *Gillette's Industrial Solution: An Account of The Evolution of The Existing Social System Together with a Presentation of an Entirely New*

Yes, this is the woke Gillette corporation whose "The Best a Man Can Get" ad campaign was discussed in Chapter 1. The Gillette razor company has embraced from its inception what historian of modern utopias Gib Prettyman has called "commercial idealism,"[12] or what I call corporate leftism.

While acknowledging the necessary role of capital for wealth production, in *The Human Drift*, Gillette railed against competition, which he believed was "the prolific source of ignorance and every form of crime, and that [which] increases the wealth of the few at the expense of the many... the present system of competition between individuals results in fraud, deception, and adulteration of almost every article we eat, drink, or wear."[13] Competition resulted in "a waste of material and labor beyond calculation."[14] Competition was the source of "selfishness, war between nations and individuals, murder, robbery, lying, prostitution, forgery, divorce, deception, brutality, ignorance, injustice, drunkenness, insanity, suicide, and every other crime, [all of which] have their base in competition and ignorance."[15] This historical text helps explain the recent Gillette ad discussed in Chapter 1; it appears that the company has finally discovered that the root of competition, and thus, of all evil, is toxic masculinity.

Gillette may as well have patented the disposable safety razor to prevent so many desperate people from cutting their throats—at least, that is, until they realized the answer to all of their problems, which he introduced in *The Human Drift*. The antidote for human suffering would be a singular monopoly, a monopoly that would "naturally" control all production and distribution, specializing in everything, such that "every article sold to consumer, from the package to its contents, will be the

---

*Remedy for the Evils It Exhibits*. The Ball Publishing Company, 1908.

12  Prettyman, Gib. "Advertising, Utopia, and Commercial Idealism: The Case of King Gillette." *Prospects*, vol. 24, 1999, pp. 231–248., at p. 232.

13  Gillette, *The Human Drift*, p. 27.

14  Ibid., p. 35.

15  Ibid.

product of the United Company, from raw material."[16] Under the United Company, the production of necessary goods, and eventually of everything, would be consolidated and centralized, eliminating the waste and hazards of the many and widely dispersed manufacturing plants and buildings of the current haphazard and chaotic system. Most cities and towns would be "destroyed," as would all competitors,[17] as the vast majority of the population would relocate to "The Metropolis," where, powered by Niagara Falls, all production would take place and everyone's lives would center around the corporation, whose commercial and governmental power would be total.

Lest one think that *The Human Drift* represented the lark of a young idealist before he came to his senses and founded a company that would attain almost unparalleled name recognition, Gillette went on to publish *"World Corporation"* in 1910, well after he patented the disposable safety razor and established a business to sell it. *"World Corporation"* was a prospectus for developing a world-wide singular monopoly, which he envisioned as a complete, and completely benevolent, economic and governmental hegemon.[18]

As to the capitalist hiatus between his socialist books, as Gillette's biographer put it, "[i]t was almost as if Karl Marx had paused between *The Communist Manifesto* and *Das Kapital* to develop a dissolving toothbrush or collapsible comb."[19] But Gillette's "commercial idealism" and innovative imagination made both his inventive business ideas and his socialist utopianism possible simultaneously. The two were inextricably wed.

In fact, despite their utterly different backgrounds and antithetical relationships to capital, Marx and Gillette both proposed a thoroughgoing socialism, differing only in terms of the means of attaining it (political versus commercial, respectively), as well as in terms of the role of and attitudes toward the capital-

---

16  Ibid., 27.
17  Ibid., 15, 27, 66, and 73.
18  Gillette, *"World Corporation"*.
19  Adams, Russell B. *King C. Gillette: the Man and His Wonderful Shaving Device*. Little, Brown, 1978, pp. 13-14.

ist class and the corporation itself.

Marx evinced a particular antipathy for the bourgeoisie, while arguably entertaining aristocratic pretentions. Although he did earn money as a freelance journalist for the *New York Tribune*, Marx owed whatever economic independence he enjoyed to the largesse of another businessman, the factory owner Friedrich Engels, who served as both patron and collaborator. One wonders whether, given the chance, Marx could have rationalized a collaboration with someone like Gillette? Quite possibly, although such corporate socialism as Gillette's had not yet fully emerged while Marx was alive.

On the other hand, while Gillette never mentioned Marx or Marxism in *"World Corporation"* or elsewhere, passages in *"World Corporation"* closely echo the Marxist understanding of history as class struggle:

> If you analyze the history of nations, you will find, no matter what their form of government, all were internally divided into two distinct classes, Rich and Poor, Masters and Slaves...[20]

Like Marx, Gillette believed that the fundamental "opposition" between owners and servants, between the consolidation of ownership in the hands of the few, and the "slavery" of the masses, must inevitably be resolved. For Marx, the "contradiction" would be overcome with "the expropriation of a few usurpers by the mass of the people,"[21] that is, the "taking back" of all productive property from the capitalist class by the otherwise dispossessed. For Gillette, it would be surpassed through the process of capitalist incorporation itself. Like Marx, Gillette believed that capital accumulation tended inexorably toward conglomeration and monopoly. The answer for Gillette was to establish a "world corporation" and offer stockholding to the masses, along with the continuous buying out of large stock

---

20 Gillette, *"World Corporation"*, p. 102.

21 Marx, Karl. *Capital: Critique of Political Economy*. The Modern Library. Vol. 1., p. 837.

holders, until all stock was held in equal shares by the denizens of the world. The process would end in socialism:

> CORPORATIONS WILL CONTINUE TO FORM, ABSORB, EXPAND, AND GROW, AND NO POWER OF MAN CAN PREVENT IT. Promoters [of incorporation] are the true socialists of this generation, the actual builders of a co-operative system which is eliminating competition, and in a practical business way reaching results which socialists have vainly tried to attain through legislation and agitation for centuries. To complete the industrial evolution, and establish a system of equity, only requires a belief in the truths herein stated—and the support of "WORLD CORPORATION."[22]

Just as Marx believed that socialism would eventually and inevitably follow from capitalism (although Marx contradicted himself on this point), so, too, did Gillette hold that the socialization of the factors of production was inevitable. In fact, for both, such socialization of production had already been accomplished. The only problem remaining was ownership and control. For Gillette, the emergence of socialism depended not on the political organization of the working masses, as it did for Marx, but rather on the commercial organization of incorporation—the continual growth of corporations, and the mergers, acquisitions, and final subsuming of all commercial interests by a single corporate monopoly, eventually owned by "the People":

> Opposition to "WORLD CORPORATION" by individuals, by states, or by governments will be of no avail. Opposition in any case can only be of temporary effect, barriers will only centralize power and cause increased momentum when they give way.[23]

The corporation would dominate material but also mental production, as Gillette praised the corporate hive mind:

---

22  Gillette, *"World Corporation"*, p. 9, emphasis in original.

23  Ibid., 62.

"WORLD CORPORATION" represents individual intelligence and force combined, centralized and intelligently directed. Individuals are OF the corporate mind, but are not THE corporate mind.[24]

And, as if anticipating Google's secret mission statement, Gillette wrote:

"WORLD CORPORATION" will possess all knowledge of all men, and each individual mind will find complete expression through the great Corporate Mind.[25]

Finally, waxing poetic in Ray Kurzweil mode, Gillette wrote:

"WORLD CORPORATION" will have life everlasting. Individual man will live his life and pass into the great beyond; but this great Corporate Mind will live on through the ages, always absorbing and perfecting, for the utilization and benefit of all the inhabitants of the earth.[26]

If this long-standing company penchant for socialist utopianism does not strike one as paradoxical and bizarre, one of Gillette's earliest ads is certainly uncanny, especially in light of the recent "We Believe" campaign. The 1905 full-color 3.5-by-5.5-inch postcard advertisement featured a "cherubic, beaming infant holding a razor, his face half-covered with shaving cream."[27] The text at the top of the postcard exhorted the shaver to "Begin Early, Shave Yourself." The ad subtly proposed a new kind of manhood (surprise!), in effect suggesting that "a man's personal freedom was compromised by the need to pay another man to shave him. At the same time, shaving could become a more telling expression of personal values if a man was potentially *responsible for shaving himself.*"[28] Shaving oneself became

---

24  Ibid., 45, emphasis in original.
25  Ibid., emphasis in original.
26  Ibid., pp. 45-46, emphasis in original.
27  Prettyman, "Advertising, Utopia, and Commercial Idealism." p. 242.
28  Ibid.

an exhibition of self-reliance and freedom but more importantly for the Gillette company, the lesson was that from infancy on men take care of themselves rather than putting the burden on their fellow men and in short reducing them to a kind of slavery.

**Figure 2-1**
**Begin Early, Shave Yourself, Gillette Safety Razor,**
**No Stropping No Honing**

It is worth noting that Gillette's business practices were not wholly at odds with the ideas in his books. True to his monopolistic impulses, he regularly filed patents, and in 1917, with the outbreak of World War I, the company provided every soldier with a shaving kit, paid for by the U.S. government.

# CHAPTER THREE

# The Digitalistas and the Digital Gulag

B Y USING THE PHRASE "digital gulag," I mean to suggest an analogy rather than an equivalence with the Soviet system. Nevertheless, the analogy should not be taken too lightly. The "totality"[1] of the Google Archipelago's reach and penetration is rather more profound than its lower-tech precursor. While generally leaving bodies intact, digital imprisonment and disappearance are no less motivated by totalitarian impulses. And the individual-as-data is easier to locate and delete than his physical counterpart.

One would be hard-pressed to find in the writing of academic digital media studies scholars—let's call them *digitalistas*—a discussion of the issues treated in this book, those most pressing to digital participants. Could the reason for that be because digitalistas, like the principals of the Google Archipelago, are also authoritarian leftists? As the French structuralist Marxist Louis Althusser argued, captives of ideology are never able to recognize their own ideological convictions *as* ideological—or, I would add, to see them as pervasive. The dominant ideology is

---

1   A favorite word of Frankfurt School theorists Theodor Adorno and Max Horkheimer, the totality refers to the whole social order, including all of its parts, and their interactions. In Adorno, Theodor W., et al. *Dialectic of Enlightenment: Philosophical Fragments*. Stanford Univ. Press, 2009, they use the word no less than fifteen times.

as invisible to believers as the air they breathe:

> ...what thus seems to take place outside ideology (to be pre-
> cise, in the street), in reality takes place in ideology. What
> really takes place in ideology seems therefore to take place
> outside it. That is why those who are in ideology believe
> themselves by definition outside ideology ...ideology never
> says, 'I am ideological'. [2]

The anti-capitalist ideology of the digitalistas blinds them to the
most salient features of the Google Archipelago, especially its
pervasive authoritarian leftism.

The digitalistas' ideology induces a hyper-vigilance regarding their primary bugbears—digital capitalist exploitation,
commodification, alienation, reification, etc.—which they see
everywhere. As they study the digital realm, the digitalistas attempt to tease out of the activities of digital media participants
an endless litany of novel anti-capitalist analyses.[3] Yet ideological sameness and uncontested premises ensure that nearly all
of the arguments are derivative and represent only minor varia-
tions on a few standard themes.

One of these standard themes combines Alvin Toffler's notion of the "prosumer"[4]—or the consumer whose consumption
amounts to production—with the Marxist theory of exploitation. According to digitalistas, with every click of a mouse or

---

2  Althusser, Louis. "Ideology and Ideological State Apparatuses (Notes
towards an Investigation)." *Ideology and Ideological State Apparatuses by
Louis Althusser 1969-70*, https://www.marxists.org/reference/archive/althuss-
er/1970/ideology.htm. (Retrieved 9 May 2019).

3  To name a few: Scholz, Trebor. "Market Ideology and the Myths of Web
2.0." *First Monday*, vol. 13, no. 3, 2008, doi:10.5210/fm.v13i3.2138; Fuchs,
Christian. "Labor in Informational Capitalism and on the Internet." *The Information Society*, vol. 26, no. 3, 2010, pp. 179–196; Fuchs, Christian. "Google Capitalism." *TripleC: Communication, Capitalism & Critique: Open Access
Journal for a Global Sustainable Information Society*, vol. 10, no. 1, 2012, pp.
42–48., doi:10.31269/triplec.v10i1.304; Robinson, Bruce. "With a Different
Marx: Value and the Contradictions of Web 2.0 Capitalism." *The Information
Society*, vol. 31, no. 1, 2014, pp. 44–51.

4  Toffler, Alvin. *The Third Wave*. William Morrow and Company, Inc., 1980.

stroke of a key, the denizens of the web are exploited by the giant digital capitalists.[5] Some digitalistas quibble over details.[6] Some disagree with the assertion regarding exploitation specifically in the digital realm as such.[7] But every digitalista, whether Marxist, neo-Marxist, or post-Marxist, must pay homage to Marxism. Everyone in the field must define his or her work in relation to Marxism, whether they are full-fledged Marxists, or not.

This is an unfortunate circumstance because the problem with the Internet is not exploitation (a notion based on the generally discredited labor theory of value), but leftist totalitarianism, of which Marxism is the main variety. Yet for every writer outside of academia who has used a term like "Google Marxism" (see the work of George Gilder, from whom I am borrowing it, and my own), hundreds of digitalistas refer to "Google capitalism," "digital capitalism," "Internet capitalism,"[8] or oth-

5  Scholz, "Market Ideology and the Myths of Web 2.0;" Fuchs, "Labor in Informational Capitalism and on the Internet;" Fuchs, "Google Capitalism; Roberts, John Michael. "Co-Creative Prosumer Labor, Financial Knowledge Capitalism, and Marxist Value Theory." *The Information Society*, vol. 32, no. 1, 2015, pp. 28–39.

6  Roberts, John Michael. "Co-Creative Prosumer Labor, Financial Knowledge Capitalism, and Marxist Value Theory." *The Information Society*, vol. 32, no. 1, 2015, pp. 28–39.

7  Banks, John, and Sal Humphreys. "The Labour of User Co-Creators." *Convergence: The International Journal of Research into New Media Technologies*, vol. 14, no. 4, 2008, pp. 401–418; Arvidsson, Adam, and Elanor Colleoni. "Value in Informational Capitalism and on the Internet." *The Information Society*, vol. 28, no. 3, 2012, pp. 135–150.

8  Fuchs, "Google Capitalism."
For uses of "digital capitalism" see for example: Fuchs, Christian, and Vincent Mosco. *Marx in the Age of Digital Capitalism*. Haymarket Books, 2017; Fuchs, Christian, and Marisol Sandoval. "Digital Workers of the World Unite! A Framework for Critically Theorising and Analysing Digital Labour." *TripleC: Communication, Capitalism & Critique. Open Access Journal for a Global Sustainable Information Society*, vol. 12, no. 2, 2014; Pace, Jonathan. "The Concept of Digital Capitalism." *Communication Theory*, vol. 28, no. 3, 2018, pp. 254–269; Schiller, Dan. *Digital Capitalism: Networking the Global Market System*. MIT, 2000; Wajcman, Judy. *Pressed for Time: The Acceleration of Life in Digital Capitalism*. The University of Chicago Press, 2016.
For uses of "Internet capitalism" see for example: Breen, Marcus. "Digital

er equivalent terms. If one had never experienced the Internet and had no other source of information to understand it other than the writing of digitalistas, one would be led to believe that cyberspace is a giant sweatshop commandeered by shop-floor managers wielding virtual whips and chains.

According to digital media studies scholars, when users open Facebook accounts, the "dumb fucks" as Mark Zuckerberg once referred to his subscribers,[9] are exploited. They freely divulge valuable demographic data, which Facebook then sells to advertisers. When they post status updates or comment on the statuses of others, Facebook users produce, without pay, the content that Facebook sells to advertisers, which means they are exploited again. When conducting web searches, the hapless and unwitting unwaged slave laborers of digital capitalism produce data that Google sells to advertisers jockeying for ranking position—exploitation![10] With almost every online activity, "[a] form of labor exploitation therefore occurs, albeit one based on voluntary and noncoerced acts of labor."[11] Or, as my favorite horror storyteller of the left, Michel Foucault puts it, albeit in the context of internalized surveillance, the unpaid digital laborer "becomes the principle of his own subjection."[12]

---

Determinism: Culture Industries in the USA-Australia Free Trade Agreement." *New Media & Society*, vol. 12, no. 4, 2010, pp. 657–676; Jin, Dal Yong. "The Construction of Platform Imperialism in the Globalization Era." *TripleC: Communication, Capitalism & Critique. Open Access Journal for a Global Sustainable Information Society*, vol. 11, no. 1, 2013, pp. 145–172; and Schröter, Jens. "The Internet and 'Frictionless Capitalism.'" *Marx in the Age of Digital Capitalism*, pp. 133–150.

9  Vargas, Jose Antonio. "The Face of Facebook: Mark Zuckerberg Opens up." *The New Yorker*, 13 Sept. 2010.

10  Fuchs, "Google Capitalism;" Mager, Astrid. "Defining Algorithmic Ideology: Using Ideology Critique to Scrutinize Corporate Search Engines." *TripleC: Communication, Capitalism & Critique. Open Access Journal for a Global Sustainable Information Society*, vol. 12, no. 1, 2014, pp. 28–39.

11  Roberts, John Michael. "Co-Creative Prosumer Labor, Financial Knowledge Capitalism, and Marxist Value Theory." *The Information Society*, vol. 32, no. 1, 2015, pp. 28–39; p. 28.

12  Foucault, Michel. *Discipline and Punish: The Birth of the Prison*. Vintage Books, 1995, p. 203.

If you think that my characterization of digitalista Marxism is exaggerated, have a peek at an essay entitled "Capitalism, Patriarchy, Slavery, and Racism in the Age of Digital Capitalism and Digital Labour," by the Marxiest of all digitalistas, Christian Fuchs. In his essay, Fuchs draws parallels—although admitting differences—between four forms of unpaid labor, three of which are "productive"—meaning that they produce commodities for sale on the market. These include housework, reproductive labor, slavery, and posting on Facebook. The following two passages are by no means ripped out of context, and therefore my quotations do not "enact violence upon the text" (nor, I should hope, on the reader):

> Slave-labour, reproductive labour and unpaid Facebook labour have in common that they are unwaged, but by being integrated into capitalist society nonetheless they create surplus-value.[13]

> Whereas the wage-worker has a contractual and legally enforceable right to be paid a wage for the performed labour, slaves, houseworkers and Facebook workers do not have such a right, which enables their exploitation as unpaid workers.[14]

Mind you, by "Facebook workers," Fuchs means anyone who uses Facebook. That includes me, for one. Have you heard enough from the digitalistas? I have.

I wrote a textbook on academic writing with two chapters on digital media and taught digital media for years. So, I knew what to expect from the academic literature when doing research for this book. Yet, in the current context (with the recent developments of banning and censorship, and the threats posed by the melding of the Google Archipelago and the state), such scholarship now reminds me of the scholasticism of Byzantine officials quibbling over trivial points of Church doctrine as the

---

13  Fuchs, Christian. "Capitalism, Patriarchy, Slavery, and Racism in the Age of Digital Capitalism and Digital Labour." *Critical Sociology*, vol. 44, no. 4-5, 2017, pp. 677–702; p. 681.

14  Ibid., p. 692.

Turks besieged Constantinople in the background—only now it is the digitalistas whose disputes involve imaginary entities. My shift in perspective was made possible by two factors. First, my politics had changed—from left communist to civil and cultural libertarian. This allowed me to notice the pervasiveness and deep penetration of leftist ideology in almost every area of life, especially academia. Second, but also in the digital landscape, the true character of Big Digital as the Google Archipelago likewise became much clearer. However, the digitalistas did not seem to notice this at all. They were busy wondering how many digital workers could be exploited simultaneously in the making of a single digital product.

The real issues lie elsewhere. While the digital realm has vastly expanded opportunities and multiplied spaces for seemingly unlimited expression, the Google Archipelago has paradoxically expedited the *disappearance* of public discursive space. First, it has increasingly rendered irrelevant any expression outside of the digital sphere. Much social life and most political discourse are now transacted in cyberspace or other digital spaces. Anyone wishing to reach an audience with a political message no longer yells from atop a soapbox in the town square—unless he's crazy. Second, because in the U.S., for example, private establishments are under no obligation to guarantee or protect the exercise of First Amendment rights—freedom of expression, freedom of religion, and the right to (virtual) assembly; therefore, they have all been effectively curtailed, especially for particular political contingents.

Thus, the agents of the Google Archipelago have had it both ways; while operating as a set of private, for-profit information and communications enterprises, they have simultaneously performed many functions typically reserved for the government. That is, the Google Archipelago is a commercial assemblage that acts increasingly like a state.

Finally, the agents of the Google Archipelago have acted like referees of a game in which they are also players, taking sides in political contests and the culture wars. The Google Archipelago exhibits blatant double standards, egregious bias, politically-motivated designations of "fake news," and tilted search engine algorithms. Clearly, the authoritarian leftism of the Google Archipelago has informed these conditions.

On the other hand, if the Google Archipelago does mark a mutation of capitalism and the birth of a new, digital capitalism, the mutation has nothing to do with new modes of surplus value extraction, or exploitation. The real issue is the "neoliberal privatization" of state functions now undertaken by the principals of the Google Archipelago, although this problem is not as the left understands it. While the public does not necessarily lose in the transfer of state services to private corporations, *the governmentalization of private enterprise* certainly poses real dangers. With the effective authority and increasing power of the state, the repressive aspects of government are retained and enhanced, while the (virtual, corporate) "state's" responsibility to the citizen remains much less than that of the traditional democratic state. The digital constellation also greatly increases the state's capacity for surveillance, information control, censorship, and the banishment or "un-personing" of *personae non gratae*, while the rights purportedly protected by the state are actually non-existent. This development is a function of the extent to which the digital giants have become *de facto* monopolies—not with the permission of the state, but as virtual proxies for it.

Since leftist ideology is dominant in academia, in the digital sphere, and just about everywhere else, digitalistas cannot see the authoritarian leftism in their midst. As stated above, ideology is invisible to those under its sway, which allows it to operate unimpeded by reality. If the digitalistas were able to recognize their own perspective as ideological, they might thereby elude ideology from time to time. But since the targets of leftist authoritarianism in the Google Archipelago are their political enemies, the digitalistas are unconcerned, even overjoyed, by such virtual disappearances. Thus, ideology operates in a feed-back loop.

Ironically, the disappearance of public space (and of people from it) had been a major concern of academic and other leftists for decades.[15] Referred to as "the commons," a phrase that metaphorically draws on the historical antagonisms between the peasantry and the Crown over the Enclosure Acts in England, public space has always been a political issue. The notion of the commons was the most powerful metaphor used by early digital utopians for describing the Internet and the World Wide Web in the 1990s.[16]

In yet another political reversal, however, akin to the new McCarthyism of the left ("it's them Russians them Russians"[17]), the issue of public space, and especially of the rights protected in it, doesn't concern leftists but rather conservatives, libertarians, and the right more broadly. At stake is the viability of their freedom of expression, right of (virtual) assembly, freedom of religion, and the right to a free press within the liberal (broadly construed) nation state.

Meanwhile, the erosion of virtual rights has only just begun. As of May 3, 2019, after banning several prominent rightwing or otherwise non-leftist figures, including Alex Jones, Milo Yiannopoulos, Paul Joseph Watson, and Laura Loomer, Facebook and its subsidiary, Instagram, promised to ban anyone they considered "dangerous"— that is, anyone to the right of Joseph Stalin. And the irony of that statement would likely be lost on Zuckerberg, a progressive for whom being virtuous literally means being politically correct, or "on the right side of history."

The developments underway should concern not only conservatives, libertarians, and right-wingers but also liberal-leftists, left-liberals, and, especially, the digitalistas. (I would add "liberals," if I thought any still existed.) Rather than arguing for and celebrating the disappearance of their political opponents from cyberspace, and thus from political relevance, as digital

---

15  Ossewaarde, Marinus, and Wessel Reijers. "The Illusion of the Digital Commons: 'False Consciousness' in Online Alternative Economies." *Organization*, vol. 24, no. 5, 2017, pp. 609–628.

16  Staff, Cacm. "Hippie Values Really Did Build the Internet." *Communications of the ACM*, vol. 61, no. 9, 2018, pp. 9–11.

17  Ginsberg, Allen. "America." *Howl and Other Poems*. City Lights, 1956, p. 33.

gatekeepers, digitalistas should be sounding alarms. As scholars of communications history, they, of all people, should know that unless this trend is thwarted and reversed, sooner or later the continually narrowing Overton window[18] will close on their very own necks.

Any student of the Soviet Union would surely recognize the pattern in play. As the history of the twentieth century vividly illustrates, when Marxism is ascendant, the "wrong" have no rights, and the number of the wrong multiplies by the day. The evidence is in: the digital gulag is under construction.

---

18  Beck, Glenn. *The Overton Window: Overton Window, Book 1*. Mercury Radio Arts, 2010.

## CHAPTER FOUR

# Digital Maoism

"A desirable text is more than a collection of accurate references. It is also an expression of personality."
— Jaron Lanier, "Digital Maoism."

"The beauty of the Internet is that it connects people. The value is in the other people. If we start to believe that the Internet itself is an entity that has something to say, we're devaluing those people and making ourselves into idiots."
— Jaron Lanier, "Digital Maoism."

"If someone's wearing a mask, he's gonna tell you the truth. If he's not wearing a mask, it's highly unlikely."
— Bob Dylan, *Rolling Thunder Review*

THE COLLECTIVISM that Jaron Lanier identified in his essay "Digital Maoism" remains a problem for the contemporary Internet.[1] Lanier refers to the issues of an over-active, over-trusted hive mind that overwrites individual voices, choices, and judgments, precisely when the individual is most

---

1   With, A Conversation, et al. "DIGITAL MAOISM: The Hazards of the New Online Collectivism." *DIGITAL MAOISM: The Hazards of the New Online Collectivism* | *Edge*, www.edge.org/conversation/jaron_lanier-digital-maoism-the-hazards-of-the-new-online-collectivism.

needed. The individual is better at making distinctions in matters of aesthetics, the design of research questions, setting the parameters within which collective choices will ultimately be determinative, and at making finer distinctions in almost every sphere of activity. Lanier provides a few examples of collectives out-performing individuals, which include grossly simplified behaviors, such as guessing the number of jelly beans in a jar. The collective is useful for determining the value of a new service or commodity, but it is not good at entrepreneurship itself. The individual cannot possibly behave as intelligently as the collective in such matters as market value, just as the collective cannot design, invent, or produce superlative art or introduce imaginative, unusual inventions or commodities—unless led by innovative individuals. One could say that individuals are better innovators and collectivities are better at providing checks against the pitfalls of individual anomalies. The collective performs well at making determinations among the possibilities devised by individual entrepreneurs. It does abysmally when attempting to devise the options from which collectivities may choose. "In other words," Lanier writes, "clever individuals, the heroes of the marketplace, ask the questions which are answered by collective behavior. They put the jellybeans in the jar." But the collective is better at guessing the number of jelly beans, once deposited.

Lanier's main focus for the hive mind and the problem of collectivism was originally *Wikipedia*. He also turned to AI, suggesting that humans are far too willing to underestimate our own intelligence in order to accord artificial intelligence to machines. But *Wikipedia* demonstrated to Lanier how collectivism especially overrides individual voices and knowledge, even when the subject of the article in question is available to contradict mistaken collective statements, as in the case of Lanier's own *Wikipedia* page.[2]

But runaway, non-directed collectivism is the least of the problems that can now be included under the heading of Digital

---

2 "Jaron Lanier." *Wikipedia*, Wikimedia Foundation, 6 June 2019, en.wikipedia.org/wiki/Jaron Lanier.

Maoism. At this juncture, the digital hive mind is directed by algorithms, agglomerated and mobilized by hashtags, and turned into the contemporary, digital equivalents of the "Church and King mobs" of the 1790s "English Terror"—to refrain from my usual references to the Red Terror, the Great Terror, or the Chinese Cultural Revolution—when the English establishment whipped plebeians into anti-Jacobin, anti-French-revolutionary frenzies that led to such attacks as the Birmingham riot of 1791.[3]

Yet today's Internet Church and King mobs imagine that they are radical, progressive, on "the right side of history," and obviously right—morally and politically, when in fact they are no better than the reactionary mobs of the past and no less under the sway of institutional and elite authority—every bit the totalitarians, if not much more so, than those whom they attack. Their belief in their righteous, social-justice probity makes them as delirious and dangerous as mobs of the past, and any consideration of them as anti-establishment is ludicrous, especially in light of the fact that they usually attack those that the Google Archipelago has deemed "dangerous" (see Chapter 6).

This chapter is not about the *Wikipedia* editorial hive mind or the Twitter mobs that are much worse, if that's possible. Instead, I adopt and expand Lanier's notion of Digital Maoism as Internet collectivism to describe the character of the technologies, technologists, and users of the Google Archipelago. But because technology is not (yet) self-generating, I examine the actions of the "woke-ers" and principals of the Digital Archipelago as well. Big Digital's woke-ers and managers cannot be ignored in a chapter on technology.

I use the term "Maoism" not to make "Mao Zedong Thought" "continuous" with "Chinese thought," not to represent the "Sinification of Marxism," not to serve as a proxy for con-

---

3 Hundreds if not thousands of sources for this material have been published. At this time, I've consulted especially Priestman, Martin. *Romantic Atheism: Poetry and Freethought, 1780-1830.* Cambridge University Press, 2006, p. 27. The crowd destroyed the meeting-house, library, and laboratory of the great astronomer and English Jacobin, Joseph Priestley. This attack led to his emigration to Pennsylvania.

temporary Chinese nationalism, and not as a global alternative to "actually-existing socialism."[4] I consider these issues to be mere matters of Marxology. They are of interest only to Marxist scholars and of no real importance, either to this book or to the politics of the future. Although, as discussed in Chapter 6, Google Marxism will likely be the ideology and social structure of the future, corporate socialism and not state socialism will be the *modus operandus*.

By "Maoism," I mean the "politico-cultural model" of Maoism, the "cultural Marxism" associated with the Chinese Cultural Revolution (1966-1976), which Sino-Marxist scholar Kang Liu suggests represented "an ideological struggle [that] turned out to be one of the greatest debacles of his [Mao's] reign."[5] With the Cultural Revolution, Mao unleashed and mobilized a fierce army of zealots, as he turned millions of students into rabid Red Guard crusaders whose mission was to purge China of classist persons and ideologies, with a goal of extirpating all tradition and convention that represented obstacles to "full communism."

The term "Digital Maoism" points to the resemblance between Maoist Cultural Revolutionary collectivism and the combined effects of digitalization and contemporary collectivism. The leftism of the Google Archipelago is functionally embedded within a whole spectrum of applications and features—including the structure of the Internet as such, the cloud, search engine algorithms, search result stacking software, web navigation tracking software, and many other applications. If or when leftist bias is not directly embedded in the software, it is superimposed by human agents. And the sentinels of surveillance and control that populate social media sites, while not technologies or bots *per se*, may as well be; they act as predictably as any technology.

General tendencies of the Google Archipelago's technologies include:

4  Liu, Kang. "Introduction: Rethinking Critical Theory and Maoism." *CLCWeb: Comparative Literature and Culture*, vol. 20, no. 3, 2018, doi:10.7771/1481-4374.3246., p. 3.
5  Ibid., p. 5.

- The algorithmic (and human-superimposed) ranking bias of Google searches in favor of liberal-to-left, as opposed to conservative websites.[6]
- Google's blacklisting of entire websites as the discovery of a file entitled "deceptive _news _blacklist _ domains.txt" demonstrates. Google's blacklisting prevents sites from showing up in special search results, including in any search features or news listings.[7]
- YouTube uses an "alternative algorithm" favoring "authoritative sources" for items manually added to a file entitled the "youtube_controversial_query_black-

6 BeauHD. "Google Search Results Have Liberal Bias, Study Finds." *Slashdot*, 22 Nov. 2016; https://news.slashdot.org/story/16/11/22/2232231/google-search-results-have-liberal-bias-study-finds; Bentley, Matt. "Google Liberal Bias: Study Shows 40% of Search Results Lean Left | CanIRank." *CanIRank Blog*, 28 Mar. 2019, www.canirank.com/blog/analysis-of-political-bias-in-internet-search-engine-results; Bolyard, Paula. "96 Percent of Google Search Results for 'Trump' News Are from Liberal Media Outlets." *Pjmedia.com*, 25 Aug. 2018, https://pjmedia.com/trending/google-search-results-show-pervasive-anti-trump-anti-conservative-bias/; Keach, Sean. "Google Accused of 'Left-Wing Bias' as Only 11% of Links Are from Right-Wing Sites." *The Sun*, The Sun, 13 May 2019, www.thesun.co.uk/tech/9062348/google-left-wing-bias-right-leaning-news/; Nicas, Jack. "Google Search Results Can Lean Liberal, Study Finds." *The Wall Street Journal*, Dow Jones & Company, 21 Nov. 2016, www.wsj.com/articles/google-search-results-can-lean-liberal-study-finds-1479760691.

7 Bloom, J. Arthur. "EXCLUSIVE: Documents Detailing Google's 'News Blacklist' Show Manual Manipulation Of Special Search Results." *The Daily Caller*, The Daily Caller, 9 Apr. 2019, https://dailycaller.com/2019/04/09/google-news-blacklist-search-manipulation/. "The deceptive_news domain blacklist is going to be used by many search features to filter problematic sites that violate the good neighbor and misrepresentation policies," the policy document says. "That document reads that it was, 'approved by gomes@, nayak@, haahr@ as of 8/13/2018.'" Ben Gomes is Google's head of search, who reports directly to CEO Sundar Pichai. Pandu Nayak is a Google Fellow, and Paul Haahr is a software engineer, whose bio on Google's internal network Moma indicates that he is also involved in, 'fringe ranking: not showing fake news, hate speech, conspiracy theories, or science/medical/history denial unless we're sure that's what the user wants.'"

list."[8] The existence of the file was revealed after a left-wing journalist for *Slate* complained when an "abortion" query on YouTube yielded anti-abortion results in top positions. An internal discussion thread was later leaked to *Breitbart News* by an anonymous Google engineer, who had marveled at YouTube's alacrity in addressing the complaint. The list revealed other political items that prompted the alternative algorithm, including "Maxine Waters," and searches for the Irish referendum to repeal that nation's Eighth Amendment, which recognized the rights of the unborn. The amendment was repealed on May 25, 2018.

• The left-leaning and differential application of Twitter policies and the disproportionate sanctioning of right and conservative users, despite comparable infraction rates for liberals and leftists.[9]

---

8  /@mikewacker. "Google's Manual Interventions in Search Results - Mike Wacker." *Medium*, Medium, 2 July 2019, https://medium.com/@mikewacker/googles-manual-interventions-in-search-results-a3b0cfd3e26c; Bokhari, Allum. "'THE SMOKING GUN': Google Manipulated YouTube Search Results for Abortion, Maxine Waters, David Hogg." *Breitbart*, 16 Jan. 2019, www.breitbart.com/tech/2019/01/16/google-youtube-search-blacklist-smoking-gun/. "The manual adjustment of search results by a Google-owned platform contradicts a key claim made under oath by Google CEO Sundar Pichai in his congressional testimony earlier this month: that his company does not "manually intervene on any search result."

9  Baumann, Beth. "Twitter Punishes Project Veritas for Exposing Pinterest's Censorship of Pro-Life Group." *Townhall*, Townhall.com, 12 June 2019, https://townhall.com/tipsheet/bethbaumann/2019/06/12/twitter-suspends-project-veritas-for-leaking-pinterests-internal-documents-classifying-ben-shapiro-as-a-white-supremacist-n2548132; Bennett, Anita. "California Congressman Devin Nunes Slaps Twitter With $250M Lawsuit Alleging Conservative Bias." *Deadline*, 19 Mar. 2019, https://deadline.com/2019/03/devin-nunes-slaps-twitter-with-250m-lawsuit-alleging-conservative-bias-1202578029/; Bourne, Lisa. "CEO Admits Twitter Is so Liberal That Its Own Conservative Employees Fear Expressing Opinions." *LifeSiteNews*, LifeSite, 18 Sept. 2018, www.lifesitenews.com/news/ceo-admits-twitter-is-so-liberal-that-its-own-conservative-employees-fear-e; Charen, Mona. "You Can't Say That on Twitter." *National Review*, National Review, 14 Feb. 2019, www.nationalreview.com/2019/02/twitter-conservative-bans-anti-free-speech/; Gobry, Pascal-Emmanuel. "Why Is Twitter Punishing Con-

- Facebook's identifying and blocking as "fake news" mostly conservative and right-leaning sources, despite significant representation of the same from the liberal-left.[10]

---

servatives?." *The Week*, 12 Jan. 2016, https://theweek.com/articles/598597/why-twitter-punishing-conservatives; Hanania, Richard. "It Isn't Your Imagination: Twitter Treats Conservatives More Harshly Than Liberals." *Quillette*, 12 Feb. 2019, https://quillette.com/2019/02/12/it-isnt-your-imagination-twitter-treats-conservatives-more-harshly-than-liberals/; Rose, Lila. "Twitter Feigns Political Neutrality, but My pro-Life Organization Sees the Bias Firsthand." *USA Today*, Gannett Satellite Information Network, 16 Sept. 2018, https://www.usatoday.com/story/opinion/voices/2018/09/16/twitter-political-bias-abortion-politics-planned-parenthood-social-media-column/1255803002/; Sheffield, Matthew. "Majority Thinks Tech Giants Are Biased against Conservatives, Poll Shows." *The Hill*, 13 Dec. 2018, https://thehill.com/hilltv/what-americas-thinking/421238-poll-majority-of-americans-think-social-media-companies-are; Stacey, Kiran. "Trump Calls in Twitter Chief to Complain about Bias." *Financial Times*, Financial Times, 23 Apr. 2019, https://www.ft.com/content/0aeb7a56-65bb-11e9-9adc-98bf1d35a056; Staff, Science X. "US Lawmaker Sues Twitter, Alleging Anti-Conservative Bias." Phys.org, Phys.org, 19 Mar. 2019, https://phys.org/news/2019-03-lawmaker-sues-twitter-alleging-anti-conservative.html.

10   Frier, Sarah. "Facebook Removed More Than 800 Accounts Spreading Fake News." Time, Time, 11 Oct. 2018, https://time.com/5422546/facebook-removes-800-fake-news-accounts/; Gryboski, Michael. "Facebook Rep Says 'Unconscious Bias' against Conservatives May Exist, Denies Intentional Bias." The Christian Post, The Christian Post, 12 Apr. 2019, www.christianpost.com/news/facebook-rep-says-unconscious-bias-against-conservatives-may-exist-denies-intentional-bias.html; Kelly, Makena. "White House Launches Tool to Report Censorship on Facebook, YouTube, Instagram, and Twitter." The Verge, The Verge, 15 May 2019, www.theverge.com/2019/5/15/18626785/white-house-trump-censorsip-tool-twitter-instagram-facebook-conservative-bias-social-media; Neikirk, Todd. "Candace Owens Is Suspended From Facebook." HillReporter.com, 17 May 2019, https://hillreporter.com/candace-owens-is-suspended-from-facebook-36133; "Stifling Free Speech: Technological Censorship and the Public Discourse | United States Senate Committee on the Judiciary." Meeting | Hearings | United States Senate Committee on the Judiciary, 10 Apr. 2019, www.judiciary.senate.gov/meetings/stifling-free-speech-technological-censorship-and-the-public-discourse; Tynan, Dan. "Facebook Accused of Censorship after Hundreds of US Political Pages Purged." *The Guardian*, Guardian News and Media, 17 Oct. 2018, www.theguardian.com/technology/2018/oct/16/facebook-political-activism-pages-inauthentic-behavior-censorship.

- Facebook and WhatsApp's policing of cyberspace and beyond to punish with banishment and legal action against violators of their terms of service, even when discovered by means of machine-learning classifiers alone.[11]
- Facebook's monitoring of both online and offline user behavior under a new "Hate organizations and their leaders and prominent members" policy.[12]
- The disproportionate banning and "shadow-banning" of right-leaning and conservative users on Twitter, Facebook, and Instagram.[13]
- The explicitly political orientation of Big Digital, as recently confirmed by the Project Veritas exposé.[14]
- The increasingly governmental functionality of Big Digital. "In the last decade, digital media platforms have grown out of their mere communication functions and

11  "WhatsApp Pledges to SUE Users over off-Platform Misbehavior." *RT International*, 11 June 2019, www.rt.com/news/461558-whatsapp-sue-off-platform-abuse/.

12  Bokhari, Allum. "Exclusive: Facebook's Process to Label You a 'Hate Agent' Revealed." *Breitbart.com*, 14 June 2019, www.breitbart.com/tech/2019/06/13/exclusive-facebooks-process-to-label-you-a-hate-agent-revealed/.

13  Ciccotta, Tom. "VICE Admits: Twitter Is Shadowbanning Conservatives, Mainstream Republicans." *Breitbart.com*, 25 July 2018, www.breitbart.com/tech/2018/07/25/vice-admits-twitter-is-shadowbanning-conservatives-mainstream-republicans/;
Savage, Michael. "Twitter Shadow Bans Michael Savage and You Might Be Next." *Newsmax*, Newsmax Media, Inc. Newsmax Media, Inc., 23 Apr. 2019, www.newsmax.com/michaelsavage/twitter-shadow-ban-algorithm/2019/04/23/id/912914/; Varney, James. "Twitter Admits Error in 'Shadow Ban' of Conservative Commentator over Lisa Page Transcript." *The Washington Times*, The Washington Times, 18 Mar. 2019, www.washingtontimes.com/news/2019/mar/18/sean-davis-shadow-ban-prompts-twitter-admission-er/; Wong, Queenie. "Twitter Faces $250 Million Lawsuit over Allegations It 'Shadow Bans' Conservatives." *CNET*, CNET, 19 Mar. 2019, www.cnet.com/news/twitter-faces-250-million-lawsuit-over-allegations-it-shadow-bans-conservatives/.

14  Ibid.

became inherently political governance systems."[15, 16]

These demonstrated tendencies mean that Big Digital represents "a set of practices, ideologies, and beliefs,"[17] not a neutral data collection and distribution system. Nor is the tendency of Big Digital toward mere tribalism *per se*, or the dominance of the Internet by the rightwing, as some digitalistas suggest, unbelievably enough.[18] Not only is the technology of Big Digital leftist; it represents a particular kind of authoritarian, globalist, identity-politics, gender-pluralist, transgender, anti-toxic-masculinist, anti-cisgender, anti-family,[19] anti-nativist, anti-conventionalist, and anti-traditionalist leftism. Particular examples of Big Digital leftism follow:

- **Covert elections rigging efforts**: In addition to meddling in the 2016 U.S. elections, Google management admitted intention to intervene in the 2020 U.S. presidential election process, under the guise of "stopping foreign interference."[20]

15   Unver, H Akin, "Digital Challenges to Democracy: Politics of Automation, Attention, and Engagement." *Journal of International Affairs*, vol. 71, no. 1, 2017, pp. 127–146; p.127.

16   Ahmed, Nafeez. "How the CIA Made Google – INSURGE Intelligence – Medium." *Insurge Intelligence*, 22 Jan. 2015, https://medium.com/insurge-intelligence/how-the-cia-made-google-e836451a959e.

17   Marwick, Alice. "Silicon Valley and the Social Media Industry." *The SAGE Handbook of Social Media*, Jean Burgess, Sage UK, 1st edition, 2017. Credo Reference, http://proxy.library.nyu.edu/login?url=https://search.credoreference.com/content/entry/sageukxgxk/silicon_valley_and_the_s ocial_media_industry/0?institutionId=57.

18   Unver, H Akin. "Digital Challenges to Democracy"; p. 128.

19   "Family and community are the last line of resistance to the state." Vlahos, Kelley Beaucar. "George Orwell's Dystopian Nightmare in China." *The American Conservative,* 24 June 2019, www.theamericanconservative.com/articles/george-orwells-dystopian-nightmare-in-china-1984/.

20   "Insider Blows Whistle & Exec Reveals Google Plan to Prevent 'Trump Situation' in 2020 on Hidden Cam." Project Veritas, www.projectveritas.com/2019/06/24/insider-blows-whistle-exec-reveals-google-plan-to-prevent-trump-situation-in-2020-on-hidden-cam/.

- **"Machine Learning Fairness"**: Google's uses "Machine Learning Fairness" to adjust for "algorithmic unfairness," defined as "unjust or prejudicial treatment of people that is related to [sic] sensitive characteristics such as race, income, [and] sexual orientation." Machine Learning Fairness adjusts for "algorithmic unfairness" by removing search results that reinforce stereotypes, even if those results may be factually accurate, as a document addressing "unjust or prejudicial treatment" and leaked by a Google insider suggests. Even when search results are factually accurate, a Google executive declared that "it may be desirable to consider how we might help society reach a more fair and equitable state, via either product intervention or broader corporate social responsibility efforts."[21] That is, non-ideologically, non-altered search results represent unfairness, while fairness is the result of informational affirmative action results manipulation.

whether or how a given algorithmic behavior should be addressed.

**If a representation is factually accurate, can it still be algorithmic unfairness?**
Yes. For example, imagine that a Google image query for "CEOs" shows predominantly men. Even if it were a factually accurate representation of the world, it would be algorithmic unfairness because it would reinforce a stereotype about the role of women in leadership positions. However, factual accuracy may affect product policy's position on whether or how it should be addressed. In some cases, it may be appropriate to take no action if the system accurately affects current reality, while in other cases it may be desirable to consider how we might help society reach a more fair and equitable state, via either product intervention or broader corporate social responsibility efforts.

**If a system's behavior is not intended, can it still be algorithmic unfairness?**
Yes. If the behavior is unfair, it meets the definition regardless of the root cause.

Figure 4-1
A Google internal document obtained by Project Veritas reveals Google's overriding of factual information to arrive at politically correct search results.

---

21  Ibid.

The use of Machine Learning Fairness to address algorithmic unfairness represents social engineering dictated by contemporary social justice objectives. Using Machine Learning Fairness, Google overwrites neutral outputs with desired results. Such search results reflect the world that Google wishes to produce rather than the world that actually exists. Google intends to "change the world," rather than merely representing it. This means that the largest information purveyor in the world has a blatant political agenda and pursues it without compunction. After all, since Google's views are indubitably "correct," why shouldn't they be promoted?

• **The biased "knowledge base" of virtual assistants,** such as Amazon's Alexa.[22]

• **New Knowledge:** a "social media 'information integrity' firm chosen by the Senate Select Committee on Intelligence to write its official report on Russian social media interference in the 2016 U.S. election was recently revealed by separate investigations of the *New York Times* and *Washington Post* to also be in the business of manufacturing fictitious Russian online support for Republican U.S. Senate candidate Roy Moore, in order to create the impression [that] he was backed by the Kremlin."[23] (More about New Knowledge in the Conclusion.)

• **Sidewalk Labs:** Alphabet's Google partner, Sidewalk Labs, plans to digitalize cities like Toronto, where "sensors would stud the Quayside development, track-

---

22 Collins, Tim. "Alexa, are you a liberal? Users accuse Amazon's smart assistant of having a political bias after she reveals she is a feminist who supports Black Lives Matter." *Daily Mail Online*, Associated Newspapers, 12 Dec. 2017, www.dailymail.co.uk/sciencetech/article-5170507/Alt-right-accuses-Amazons-Alexa-liberal-political-bias.html.

23 "Kremlin-Supported: How the Experts at New Knowledge Manufacture Fictitious Russians for an Eager Corporate Media and Retain Their Credibility." *The Raucous Rooster,* 28 Feb. 2019, theraucousrooster.com/2019/02/27/kremlin-supported-how-the-experts-at-new-knowledge-manufacture-fictitious-russians-for-an-eager-corporate-media-and-retain-their-credibility/.

ing everything from which street furniture residents use to how quickly they cross the street...Sidewalk would need funding commitments and regulation changes from many layers of Canadian government," which demonstrates the increasingly governmental presumptions of Big Digital.[24]

•   **Smart Cities**: inaugurated in Shenzhen, China, smart cities use cameras, ambient Wi-fi, LED lights, CCTVs, virtual fences, cell-phone monitoring, and other digital tracking mechanisms for surveillance and control of smart city inhabitants. Fifty Chinese cities are already "smart" and Darwin, Australia has adopted the program for their own "safety." (See Chapter 7: AI with Chinese Characteristics.)[25]

•   **Meghan Murphy**: a feminist writer and "TERF" (so-called "trans-exclusionary, radical feminist"), referred to Jonathan Yaniv as "he" in a tweet. Yaniv had been making appointments with female beauticians in Vancouver, asking for a "Brazilian bikini wax." "He" subsequently brought sixteen Vancouver beauticians before the British Columbia grand jury after they refused to service "him" because of "his" male genitalia.

•   **Laura Loomer**: Banned for life from Twitter for a tweet criticizing Ilhan Omar (U.S. Representative, MN) and Sharia Law, Loomer has since been banned from all

---

24 Marshall, Aarian. "Alphabet's Plan for Toronto Depends on Huge Amounts of Data." Wired, Conde Nast, 25 June 2019, http://www.wired.com/story/alphabets-plan-toronto-depends-huge-amounts-data/;
Unver, H Akin. "Digital Challenges to Democracy: Politics of Automation, Attention, and Engagement.." *Journal of International Affairs*, vol. 71, no. 1, 2017, pp. 127–146: "In the last decade, digital media platforms have grown out of their mere communication functions and became inherently political governance systems" (p. 127).

25 Vlahos, Kelley Beaucar. "George Orwell's Dystopian Nightmare in China." *The American Conservative*, 24 June 2019, www.theamericanconservative.com/articles/george-orwells-dystopian-nightmare-in-china-1984/;
Philipp, Joshua. "China's Big Brother Social Control Goes to Australia." *The Epoch Times*, 30 Apr. 2019, www.theepochtimes.com/chinas-big-brother-social-control-goes-to-australia_2898104.html.

major social media platforms.

• **Julian Assange:** Remains unverified on Twitter despite his enormous international stature and 211,000-plus followers. Assange represents an example of Big Digital's functionality as a state apparatus, given that Assange is considered a counter intelligence agent.

• **"Learn to Code":** Several conservatives were banned from Twitter for ironically using the phrase "Learn to Code" in response to laid-off leftist journalists. Meanwhile, it was leftist journalists who first used the sarcastic admonition when the journalists aimed the phrase at working-class Trump voters who lost their jobs to automation. "Learn to Code" was what the journalists advised the newly unemployed.

• **Antifa:** a known leftist terrorist group, Antifa has not been banned from Twitter, but the "Proud Boys," brainchild of Gavin McInnes, have been banned from all major social media platforms, as has McInnes himself.

• **Steven Crowder:** Arguably the biggest conservative voice on YouTube, Crowder was demonetized after *Vox* activist Carlos Meza created a montage of Crowder's comedic political commentary. In the footage, Crowder calls Carlos Maza a "lispy queer" (Maza refers to himself as queer). "Adpocalypse" for independent media across the platform was the result.

• **Covington Catholic High School Students:**
  * **Kathy Griffin** tweeted an open call to dox the Covington students—a blatant violation of Twitter policies—without consequence.
  * **Reza Aslan:** A self-described "internationally renowned writer, commentator, professor, producer, and scholar of religions," tweeted, "Honest question, have you ever seen a more punchable face than this kid's?" The tweet referred to seventeen-year-old Covington Catholic High School student, Nicholas Sandmann, who, when he and

fellow classmates were menaced on the steps of the Lincoln Memorial by Native American activist Nathan Phillips and other leftist agitators, stood by stoically and smiled. The tweet remains on Twitter and Mr. Aslan retains Twitter's verified status.

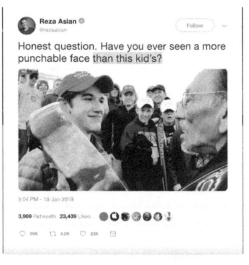

**Figure 4-2**
**Tweet by Reza Aslan directed at a High School Student Nicholas Sandmann suggesting that his face is "punchable." Such remarks from a "scholar of religions" would be ironic if not for the fact that for decades religious studies has been a secular field with no regard for religious or moral observance.**

Aslan's most renown book, *Zealot: The Life and Times of Jesus of Nazareth* (2014), casts Jesus Christ as one among many nationalist, political Israeli zealots—an unoriginal thesis that may as well have been gleaned from Monty Python's satirical *Life of Brian* (1979). Aslan's "scholarship" hasn't been considered worthy of review by any of the top religious studies journals, and the lower-tier journals that have reviewed his work have scoffed at its discredited, outdated, and tendentious polemics. Although a scholarly joke, *The New Yorker* declared Aslan's *Zealot* "Riveting ...

Aslan synthesizes Scripture and scholarship to create an original account." *The Los Angeles Times* called
*Zealot* a "A lucid, intelligent page-turner."[26]

* Uncle Shoes (@HouseShoes), a hip-hop DJ, un-
hinged leftist and verified Twitter user tweeted about
the Covington students: "LOCK THE KIDS IN THE
SCHOOL AND BURN THAT BITCH TO THE
GROUND." Mr. Shoes also called for mass shootings
of Trump supporters in a series of tweets: "If you are
a true fan of Shoes I want you to fire on any of these
red hat bitches when you see them. On sight." He remains a verified Twitter account holder.

**The Making, Manipulation, and Diversion of Digital
Hive Minds**

Much has been made of Google's historical ties to the U.S.
intelligence community (IC) and military research agencies. In
the 1990s, the IC saw the Internet as an unprecedented source
for harvesting actionable intelligence, while military research
agencies recognized its potential for new data-driven warfare

---

26  "About." Reza Aslan, http://rezaaslan.com/about/. (See "About." Reza
Aslan, http://rezaaslan.com/book/zealot-the-life-and-times-of-jesus-of-naz-
areth/.) Meanwhile, a serious scholarly examination of the book in *Critical
Research on Religion*, suggests otherwise: "The lack of critical analysis of
sources and the periodic historical confusions in his narrative, however,
suggest that *Zealot* is not a historical investigation. The biography at the
end of the book explains that his formative training was in fiction and that
his academic position is in the teaching of creative writing." In other words,
Aslan's *Zealot* is a piece of sheer fiction and the real zealot here is Aslan
himself. No wonder he's managed to fool the fake reviews departments and
fake scholarship departments of the Google Archipelago. "Aslan's degrees
include a Bachelor of Arts in Religious Studies from Santa Clara University
(Major focus: New Testament; Minor: Greek), a Master of Theological Studies from Harvard University (Major focus: History of Religions), a PhD in
the Sociology of Religions from the University of California, Santa Barbara
(http://rezaaslan.com/about/. See Horsley, Richard. "Reza Aslan, *Zealot: The
Life and Times of Jesus of Nazareth*." *Critical Research on Religion*, vol. 2, no.
2, 2014, pp. 195–205., doi:10.1177/2050303214535006, p. 195.

systems.[27] With only their human-based methods, the IC could not approach let alone make sense of the mass of data the generated on the Internet.

Cultivating the information age from its infancy, the IC and military agencies invested in university research and entrepreneurial innovation to achieve their ends. Faced with an otherwise unintelligible dross of data, they farmed-out the information gathering and analysis of intelligence work, and the information warfare aspects of military strategy, to the advanced developers of information systems in and around Stanford and the wider Silicon Valley.

The Manhattan Project, satellite technology, the aeronautics industry, and the Internet were earlier examples of such collaborations. In fact, although "[m]any people think that the dependence of the university on government and private support for research emerged only in the wake of World War II and the Cold War, … the dependence on external research funding began in earnest during World War I."[28] Yet prospects for Internet surveillance certainly fomented distrust.[29] The Joint Enterprise Defense Initiative (JEDI) will prove no less collaborative.[30]

Ironically, those most likely to protest collaboration between state, corporate, and research institutions—namely, leftists—have been rendered inert by Big Digital, which agglomerates and folds them into complicit and politically quiescent

---

27  Ahmed, Nafeez. "How the CIA Made Google - INSURGE Intelligence." *Medium*, INSURGE Intelligence, 13 Nov. 2015, https://medium.com/insurge-intelligence/how-the-cia-made-google-e836451a959e; Nesbit, Jeff, and Jeff Nesbit. "Google's True Origin Partly Lies in CIA and NSA Research Grants for Mass Surveillance." *Quartz*, Quartz, 8 Dec. 2017, https://qz.com/1145669/googles-true-origin-partly-lies-in-cia-and-nsa-research-grants-for-mass-surveillance/.

28  Shumway, David. "The University, Neoliberalism, and the Humanities: A History." *Humanities*, vol. 6, no. 4, 2017, pp. 83–92.

29  Ahmed, Nafeez. "How the CIA Made Google."

30  "[A] cloud computing platform that will eventually run much of the Pentagon's digital infrastructure—from data storage to image analytics to the translation of intercepted phone calls." Silverman, Jacob. "Tech's Military Dilemma." *The New Republic*, 7 Aug. 2018, https://newrepublic.com/article/148870/techs-military-dilemma-silicon-valley.

collectives. Big Digital has wooed and won over an otherwise obstreperous and oppositional political contingent by massifying and encouraging their group-self-conscious identification and constantly reflecting their values back to them. As if by Pavlovian conditioning, when leftists participate in a collective, they associate their participation with activism. Big Digital Maoism deceives the left into believing that it is engaging in activism, precisely as it plays the part of enthusiastic and unwitting shill for the agenda of the corporate, globalist corporation. Collectivism is so central to leftism that I have sometimes wondered whether it represents the true end, rather than merely the means, of leftist politics. That is, rather than a means for applying mass political pressure to achieve particular goals, what if collectivism itself is the ultimate goal? Collectivism may have originated as an adaptive function developed for the protection of individuals who feel overpowered by dominant opponents.

The left derides anything standoffish or singular. Even Lanier's reference to a singular "hive mind" drew the ire of critics, who insisted that there are many and sundry hive minds.[31] But Lanier's point was not that there can be only one hive mind but rather that all hive minds, regardless of their differences, share the same set of hive-mind traits. The primary trait of the hive mind is group-self-consciousness. "We don't have to think, therefore we are right" is the collectivist equivalent of Cartesian self-affirmation.

As The People Who Know Everything, Google and YouTube must have a good reason for their exclusive policing of "right-wing extremism." It is likely one of its many tactics for building a massified constituency. YouTube's blogs and policies about eliminating "hate speech," for example, practically equate all hate speech with expressions of "supremacy."[32] While this may

---

31 Tumlin, Markel, et al. "Collectivism vs. Individualism in a Wiki World: Librarians Respond to Jaron Laniers Essay 'Digital Maoism: The Hazards of the New Online Collectivism.'" *Serials Review*, vol. 33, no. 1, 2007, pp. 45–53., doi:10.1080/00987913.2007.10765092.

32 "Our Ongoing Work to Tackle Hate." Official YouTube Blog, 5 June 2019, youtube.googleblog.com/2019/06/our-ongoing-work-to-tackle-hate.html.

suggest a blissful ignorance of history—that four times as many innocent people have been killed in the name of "equality" than in the name of "supremacy"—one shouldn't discount the digital giants' omniscience. Certainly, the YouTube and Google hive mind knows.

But how is such asymmetry rationalized? What is the tacit explanation? Rightist ideology is policed because it is deemed "problematic" (politically wrong and thus morally evil). Leftist ideology, on the other hand, is given a free pass because it obviously poses no danger. YouTube and other Big Digital principals represent leftism—to themselves and their constituencies—as the default no-fault political belief system. While the crimes of right-wing political villainy are kept in circulation and regularly denounced, the left's political crimes, despite its much larger number of victims, are swept under the carpet, ignored, or justified. YouTube regards leftist ideology as obviously benign but also naturally beneficial. The moral probity of leftism is taken for granted. Leftists are on "the right side of history," even though their historical crimes are unparalleled.

What is accomplished by such whitewashing of leftism? In addition to producing and cementing its digital hive-minded collectives, by disappearing leftist criminality, Big Digital eludes criticism of its own authoritarian leftism. Just as King Camp Gillette couched his megalomania and dictatorial ambitions in a rhetoric of equality and altruism (see Chapter 2), so Big Digital's leftism has provided a mantle of virtue (transparent to some) to mask its dictatorial practices. As such, the principals of Big Digital have managed to divert attention and deflect criticism from their global monopolist and governmental ambitions.

## CHAPTER FIVE

# Inside the (Digital) Gulag

"[I]t takes a great ideal to produce a great crime."
—Martin Malia. *The Soviet Tragedy*

"Be realistic: Demand the impossible!"
— Slogan of the student rebellion, Paris, France, May 1968

"It ain't 2009 no more/Yeah, I know what's behind that door."
— Mac Miller, "2009"

### A Defector in California

O N THE AFTERNOON of May 9, 1968, a non-descript seventy-six-year-old Russian man—a former low-level Communist Party member, a technician in the People's Commissariat of Machine Tools, a Gulag prisoner, and a defector—was paid a visit at his bungalow in Mountain View, California. The devil, you'll see, is in the details.

Over thirty years before, on January 29, 1937, on an otherwise unremarkable day—beyond, that is, overlapping with the third of the three very public Moscow trials—he emitted some twenty seconds of barely audible grumbling at an inopportune time and within earshot of an NKVD officer. His otherwise inconsequential grousing proved decisive. Unbeknownst to him,

93

he was placed on a list of "socially dangerous elements." "Right deviationist" was the particular designation written in the column to the right of his name.

On February 9, 1937, in the middle of the night, he was arrested. Soon the Gulag camp surrounded him.

Exactly five years later to the day, his confinement ended as abruptly and inexplicably as it began. His sentence had been served and he was released.

He returned to his hometown of Orenburg and thought he no longer recognized it. It didn't occur to him that he could no longer recognize as himself the self that had once lived there.

Unrecognizable, he would defect.

Although he'd endured five years of arbitrary and pointless cruelty at the hands of his comrade-persecutors, he found escaping belief much more difficult than scaling the metaphorical Iron Curtain, whose inside was covetously guarded by a line of resolute sentinels believing that any slippage through the Berlin wall near the city center meant their death—and it did. But our defector reduced the number of potential executions by not attempting to escape on foot. Instead, he became cargo. A childhood friend had become a pilot with Aeroflot, the only Soviet airline, and with flights that carried only cargo. He managed to convince his friend to transport him out of the country. He was stowed in a wooden crate and loaded into a plane headed for Riga, the capital of Latvia.

In an airport hangar, his childhood friend pried open the wooden box where he'd lain motionless.

Now, from a "safe distance," he saw the entirety of his existence in a new light. Whatever he had believed, he believed because not believing meant ceasing to exist. What was best to believe? It depends. On what? On the consequences of not believing. But what did belief guarantee? Nothing, to be precise. Why nothing? Because one's belief ensured nothing about the belief of others. Their beliefs could suddenly change. Or their shared belief might eventually reveal itself as a mass delusion, and no one is safe in a state of collective insanity.

He sought asylum. The U.S. granted it in 1948 and he was

among the first defectors from the heart of the Soviet Union. Soon after lighting in New York, he moved, town by city, city by town, hop-scotching from the East Coast to the Midwest, from Midwest to the West Coast. He finally stopped in San Francisco's South Bay on the first of October 1949.

He applied for a General ham radio operator's license in December and received it in early January. By February 1950, he began a career as an outspoken, yet somewhat obscure, ham radio operator. He used his channel to unleash fierce criticism on the Soviet Union and communism in general. But soon he was captivated by the elements of the communist left in America.

By 1952, coincident with the start of the McCarthy hearings, American communism had become his obsession. He paid no attention to the hearings, but from what he gleaned off-handedly, he considered them completely off-base.

His obsession eventually escaped his skull and expressed itself in nervous tics, stuttering, and itching. His tongue would not stay put in his mouth, and he licked his lips or lodged his tongue in one or the other corner on the outside of his mouth. He stuttered when his utterances began with the definite article "the." In bed, the obsession metamorphosed into invisible, weightless bugs that detonated, scattering itch-bombs all over his body. When he tried to obliterate one by scratching, it instantly leaped to another part of his body and exploded, scattering more itch bombs. An itch jumped from the inside of an eyelid to the arch of a foot, from the back of an ear and into the opposite nostril, from a spot on the head to a crease behind a knee, always eluding him. It was a torture as arbitrary as the Gulag.

One detail has been omitted thus far; were it not for the abomination of something like the preternaturally flying invisible virus of communism, to which he failed to develop a complete immunity, he might easily have equaled or surpassed Solzhenitsyn's literary accomplishments, and preceded him as well. No, the necessary environmental conditions for his talent to sprout as if by spontaneous generation had not been lacking. He was not rye that might have become barley, barley that might have been transformed into wheat—given the right diet of sun, water, and soil. As it turns out, the English Romantic poets were right and the social environmentalists were wrong—genius is born, not made.

No, he inherited his genius and it existed. It was just that no one else could see it because he did not materialize it for anyone but himself. He'd kept notebooks, accumulating since the first week of his internment, now several feet high. He'd written at length about spontaneous order and its superiority to the human superimposition of order. This led him into economic, scientific, technological and theological discussions. Although the topics were philosophical, the writing itself was the dramatic, rhythmic, and beautifully descriptive prose we find in the best fiction. Curiously, he'd never written a word on his own accord before his first entry in the Gulag.

If only I could make them see, really see!

A communist world would always remain, and remain an always-receding ideal to which people would be drawn from anywhere, an ideal to and for which they might more easily be sacrificed.

In a dream, he's in the basement of the Social Engineering section of the Social Science library at UC Berkeley, gathered around a carrel talking with a small group of young communists in hushed tones. One might be the young Bob Avakian, before he became the leader of Revolutionary Communist Party, USA—only he's somehow older, with graying blond hair, a big gut, and wearing a Hawaiian shirt. The valence of the persuasion slowly begins to shift, coming his way from them. Surely, he thought, a former believer—imprisoned by the executors of a belief and executioners of people on behalf of a belief, who, when released became an apostate, then a defector, and finally an asylum-seeker—could never again be drawn, tricked by unexpected believers on the other side of the wall. Would he relinquish his "petty bourgeois" cottage in the sun, risking a second sentence in the shades of the Gulag? He knew so absolutely that the answer was "no," that that knowledge turned into its opposite on the inside of his skull.

"On!" he woke up screaming. In a feverish sweat, he snapped his body into an "L", his upper-torso upright. Had this "really happened," he wondered, or was it "only a nightmare," like those he had had after graduating college? He was six-foot-tall and back in primary school again, learning the alphabet.

Despite moving so far from the Gulag, he'd actually drawn nearer to it. Or rather he'd beckoned it to follow him. Once the Gulag, always the Gulag. Even as the horrors leached out in reports after Nikita Khrushchev's not-so "Secret Speech,"[1] which began to reach the rest of the world from the early 1960s,[2] it seemed to elude those around him—other than those captivated by it, those who became believers and then proselytizers, young and angry fanatics, and the old guard that never gives up.

By early 1968, he realized that political ideologies were much like computer code, if indeed they weren't expressed precisely in computer code. The U.S. variant of the communist code was a bug, a piece of code that insinuated itself into the operating system and took it over. Buried deep within the kernel of the belief resided the piece of code that called for its self-replication—that said, in effect, "copy and distribute me."

The first symptom of the bug was the fixation on the visionary ideal. The visionary ideal was, previous to admission into one's consideration, an itinerant and homeless vagabond. But once gaining entrance, which required only the slightest assent, it assumed the deportment of a king annexing new territory,

---

1 Edele, Mark. *The Soviet Union* (Wiley Short Histories) (pp. 159-161). Wiley. Kindle Edition.

2 Khlevniuk, Oleg V. *The History of the Gulag: From Collectivization to the Great Terror*. Stalin Digital Archive. New Haven: Yale University Press, 2004. Stalin Digital Archive. @01 Web. 27 May 2019, pp. x-xii. Khlevniuk points out that with the Soviet denials and misrepresentations of the Gulag system and the "Gulag-deniers" in the West, knowledge of the system had been more or less successfully suppressed through the 1950s. But by 1962, with the publication of Aleksandr Solzhenitsyn's *One Day in the Life of Ivan Denisovic*, "[a]s Galina Vishnevskaya put it, the genie was out of its bottle, and no one could put it back ... Solzhenitsyn's *Gulag Archipelago, 1918–1956*—another one not published in the USSR itself—effectively destroyed doubts and delusions in the West (it is reported to have effected a radical change in the French intelligentsia in particular)."

sprawling out and appropriating more and more unto itself. The newly occupied mind swelled with the certainty of the possibility and the moral necessity of the ideal's realization. Encoded nearby was yet another set of instructions, which called for the vision's execution at all costs, overwriting any objections that might arise.

A secondary executable in the communism software suite potentiated eloquence and persuasiveness whenever the slightest talent was available for incorporation, propelled by an urgent yet rhythmic delivery system the likes of which had never stopped echoing in his ears, not even within the Gulag's core. Once initiated, the executable set in motion processes and enabled features that were not easily disabled. Force alone was insufficient to make them stop—anything short of deadly force, that is. And even then, the processes might leap to a nearby host before the first host died.

Wrapped within the larger code, you found the piece of code that triggered an urgency. The urgency had two parts—the first to make escape necessary and the second to impose a belief in its possibility. But the urgency was agnostic. It was a blind urgency to exchange current conditions for those of another place, another system, another world, regardless of the differences. For socialism, the urgency represented an initial advantage. It covered socialism's many obvious weaknesses, which would become apparent upon closer inspection, but which the urgency prevented. Again, referring to the U.S. variant of communist code, without the urgency, you would think twice about exchanging a world where you could choose between fifteen brands of toothpaste for a system that made only one (if that), a world that permitted you to seek a job from among hundreds or thousands on offer and from among several careers, for a system in which your job was assigned to you by the state, a world in which you might vote for the opponent of the current leader (even though both might be lousy), for a system under which only one political party was legal, a world in which you might manage to buy a small house or even a small family farm, for a system in which you'd be shot in the head if you refused to give up your house or farm, a world where you could express odd opinions or even revolutionary ideas and simply be criticized or ignored, for a system in which such an infraction would land you in a prison camp or deliver a bullet to the head.

If not for the urgency, the core executable socialist code otherwise would be overwritten by such considerations. But the inclusion of the urgency as part of the socialist program suite interfered with any such analysis. Yet socialists often produced brilliant analyses within a closed set of possibilities.

The agnosticism of the urgency, its utter blindness, could also act as a bug within a bug. It could work in reverse of the ideal. It could rebel against the master code, reversing the dialectic. It could make one desperate to escape a socialist world and to believe escape possible. The thesis and antithesis could be reversed so that instead of the antithesis negating capitalism it could instead negate the negation, socialism.[3] How the urgency can change directions within an otherwise closed-system loop is beyond anyone's comprehension at present.

But now, he was the urgency, His urgency acted as a counter to the urgency of the communists, whom he met in the Bay area and on the ham radio channels. He was the negation of their

---

3 The "negation of the negation" is a philosophical notion that Marx derived from Georg Wilhelm Friedrich Hegel's dialectical methods. For communism, the capitalist represents the negation of the individual owner of small, petty property, the result of his own individual labor. This property relation is negated by the capitalist whose ownership represents a massive appropriation of the property of many others and its ownership by a small capitalist class possessing enormous wealth. Thus, capitalism is the negation of earlier property relations. Socialism is the negation of capitalism and thus the negation of the negation of capitalism. Marx put it as follows in *Das Kapital*: "It is the negation of negation. This [socialism] re-establishes individual property, but on the basis of the acquisitions of the capitalist era, i.e., on co-operation of free workers and their possession in common of the land and of the means of production produced by labour. The transformation of scattered private property, arising from individual labour, into capitalist private property is, naturally, a process, incomparably more protracted, arduous, and difficult, than the transformation of capitalistic private property, already practically resting on socialised production, into socialised property." Quoted in Frederick Engels. *1877: Anti-Duhring - XIII. Negation of the Negation*, www.marxists.org/archive/marx/works/1877/anti-duhring/ch11.htm.

urgency, and since their urgency represented a negation of the current system, he was the negation of the negation. He knew the dialectical thinking better than they did, which wasn't saying much. He used the Hegelian method against communism, dialectical thinking against dialectical formulae.

Finding communists out here, on this misty peninsula perched over the edge of the earth, he became convinced that more than a few people existed who were capable of becoming the jailers and mass murderers of "the people," the same people for whom they would take over the world, given the people's support, or at least a lack of sufficient opposition. Only one group could accomplish it at a time, and, as if to demonstrate the precise obverse of the communist creed—one person within that group would take a dominant position—all on a promise that he would hand state power back to them, in the end.

Meanwhile, the talents of our Soviet defector hadn't gone completely unnoticed. For one, his radio channel had its share of listeners, including those interested in his activities from a strategic point of view—state agents and members of various parties and sects. An émigré from the Soviet Union, he naturally drew such attention. Despite or even because of his conspicuous anti-Soviet screeds, agents monitored his ham radio channel closely and followed his incursions into leftist and communist circles, including his meeting with top Communist Party USA (CPUSA) figures. These same agents had made sure that his application for a General ham operator's license had been rushed through the Federal Communications Commission (FCC). As if tearing a page from a Cheka playbook, a few agents said that they preferred potential political opponents to operate in the open so that any subversion might be more easily detected.[4]

The obvious concern with such a vocal defector was that he

---

4 "Instead of merely outlawing these parties, which would simply force them underground and make them even more difficult to control, it seems preferable to grant them a sort of semi-legal status. In this way we can have them at hand, and whenever we need to we can simply pluck out troublemakers, renegades, or the informers that we need…" Qtd. in Courtois Stéphane, and Mark Kramer. *The Black Book of Communism: Crimes, Terror, Repression.* Harvard University Press, 2004, p. 85.

protested too much. One had to consider the possibility that his radio activity represented a cover for Soviet espionage, collaboration, advising, or all three. Contrary to the received notion that McCarthyism and the Red Scare were overblown, those with knowledge of the depth and extent of Western involvement in the Russian revolution and its aftermath could tell you that Uncle Joe got it wrong. The Soviets themselves could not have done better propaganda-wise if they had staged the McCarthy hearings themselves. Narrowly focused on "communist sympathizers" and "party members," McCarthy made concern about communism appear hysterical, while vastly underestimating the depth and penetration of socialist-communist ideology in almost every area of culture and society.[5]

Late in the afternoon of May 9, 1968, as the student rebellion reached its peak in France, two grey-suited men wearing fedoras appeared as conspicuously inconspicuous as they possibly could as they arrived at our former-Soviet's cottage and stood before his front door. After a few seconds, and upon noting the other one nod, one of the men took hold of the horse-shoe-shaped brass knocker attached to the jaws of the brass lion head

---

5 "Reaction to the excesses of the McCarthy era has also confused the debate over historical issues surrounding American communism, particularly in regard to its clandestine activities. Because McCarthy and those like him used the issue of American Communist involvement in Soviet espionage to assail liberals and Democrats, some people concluded that anyone who suggested that the CPUSA was involved in covert activities and espionage was a McCarthyite—McCarthy's guilt-by-association technique in reverse. To recognize the excesses, mistakes, and injustices of McCarthy's anti-Communist crusade is not to accept the distorted view that anticommunism was an irrational and indefensible persecution of a group of American reformers or that it was impossible for the CPUSA to have been engaged in nefarious activities. Indeed, the documents in this volume demonstrate that the widespread popular belief that many American Communists collaborated with Soviet intelligence and placed loyalty to the Soviet Union ahead of loyalty to the United States was well founded. Concern about the subversive threat of the CPUSA and worries that Communists employed in sensitive government jobs constituted a security risk were equally well founded." Klehr, Harvey, Haynes, John Earl and Firsov, Fridrikh Igorevich. *The Secret World of American Communism*. Stalin Digital Archive. New Haven: Yale University Press, . Stalin Digital Archive. Web. 17 Jul 2019, p. 16.

and struck the brass plate with it three times. No answer. They waited a few seconds. Then the other of the two men took hold of the knocker and stuck the brass plate, only much more forcefully and many more times than his compeer had. The problem wasn't that the former Soviet citizen was not home but rather that he had been giving a lengthy and impassioned speech on his ham radio channel. He was in the back of the small house and didn't hear the knocking.

The two men figured as much and went to the back door. One of the two used his right hand as an additional visor and looked through the glass window of the back door. He saw our man sitting at his kitchen table, yelling and gesticulating. The same man knocked on the glass of the back door. To say that our former Soviet citizen was startled would be an understatement. He dropped the handheld device onto the table, threw his hands into the air, and screamed: "*Sdayus! Sdayus!*" ("I surrender! I surrender!")

The agent gestured, as if closing a window made of air, to say, "Relax. We're not here to arrest you."

Our former Soviet citizen caught his breath, looked at the men steadily, then proceeded to unlock and open the door.

The agents introduced themselves as "Agent 1" and "Agent 2." After very limited small talk, Agent 1 broached the reason for the visit.

This is what our former Soviet thought he heard Agent 1 say: "Imagine a version of your former self—still in the Gulag and still a zealous Soviet communist. Traumatized since his improbable and incomprehensible arrest five years earlier, your former self remains incognizant of the fact that his residence is the Gulag and his occupancy an internment. Psychologically speaking, he is afflicted with a dissociative disorder, in particular, partial dissociative amnesia. His memory stops at precisely 3:33 AM, February 9, 1937.

"By means of an extremely advanced and secret military technology that will not be released to the public for at least seventy-five years, you are able to visit your former self in the Gulag, or a possible version of your former self."

As it turned out, the agency liked what they'd heard from and about our former Soviet citizen. They had begun to consider him an asset some time ago. And they thought he might be the perfect guinea pig to test a new, "revolutionary" technology—likewise, to engage in a completely unimaginable high-tech form of espionage. The technology is a televisual communications system, like the current-day Skype (May 2019), yet with access to a digitized past that will allow the user, so the agency believes, to meaningfully engage in "real time" with a possible past. What, if anything, will the contemporary self say to his former self, given the certain knowledge that the latter's release—either from the Gulag or from the ideology— is by no means guaranteed by the future?

To be continued…

## The Digital Gulag

The Soviet encounter above—between the former self in the Gulag and the present self who will visit him—is parallel to the encounter described next. The speaker in the following passages, identified in Facebook statuses, is represented in the digital traces of my former, communist-believing self. Running a 2009 version of the U.S. variant of the communist code, he is the analog of his former Soviet self still imprisoned in Soviet Gulag. The commentator and analyst of these passages is the analog of the freed, defected, emigrated, former Soviet self. The analogy also corresponds to two perspectives or views of the Google Archipelago; the emigrated Soviet self, living in Mountain View, California, and the doubly imprisoned former self still in the Gulag correspond to two views of the Google Archipelago—a view from "outside" and a view from "inside," respectively. I place "outside" and "inside" quotation marks to suggest that the distinction between the two positions is uncertain where the Google Archipelago is concerned. Is an "outside" perspective of the Google Archipelago possible? Finally, the analogy applies to those who see the Google Archipelago and the many who do not. The four pairs—past and present, digital and corporeal, inside and outside, non-seeing and seeing—are often but not necessarily separated spatially. The question is whether or not they will forever remain *ideologically* separated. The answer may have world-historical[6] significance. One member of each pair cannot see the gulag, while the other member is incapable of forgetting it. Of course, this raises the question: which is the prisoner?

### Digital Retraces

Michael Rectenwald
May 6, 2010 ·
Fear of flying, of losing attachments, of soaring above earth as in my dream a few nights ago, when I flew of my own accord, sailing a-way above earth through clouds, high winds, storms and meteor and asteroid showers, my youngest son holding onto my back for dear life, unable to land.

This dream expresses a fear of losing attachments to my family and other relationships grounded in the familiar and as distinct from the "clouds, high winds, storms and meteor and asteroid showers," or what to the rest of my family was an alien atmosphere. To make sure I didn't lose all familial attachments, I took my youngest son, the most impressionable of my children, with me.

Michael Rectenwald
May 10, 2010 at 10:05 AM ·
My dream last night: I'm undergoing a test of mind and body apparently conducted by some official institution. I'm in a swinging chair atop a giant lift as if on a pole. I have to answer questions. The examiner keeps score. At some point, I realize that the examination is not "objective" but that the rightness or wrongness of the answers falls to the examiner's discretion

---

6  The adjective "world-historical" has been used by Marxists, often to refer to the significance of the working class. But the coinage was Samuel Taylor Coleridge's, a convert to conservatism, who used it in his notebooks in 1833: Coleridge, Samuel Taylor. *The notebooks* (ed. Kathleen Coburn), 1st edition, 1957–2002 (5 vols. in 10).

[more to follow]...

Michael Rectenwald
May 10, 2010 at 10:07 AM ·
I realize that I'm giving right answers but that the examiner is not counting them as "right." Then I remember yelling, "I'm right, you're just too stupid to know it" in the examiner's face. I am being tested physically as well, having to swing way up and maintain a perfectly aligned arc. Continued...

Michael Rectenwald
May 10, 2010 at 10:09 AM ·
At this point I realize I'm actually being tortured. I escape somehow, running through woods and small buildings of a sort of encampment. I fly out of this small town above the main street. I then meet family and we enter door after door. One leads to another country—Germany. Also, later, I realize I've traveled through time into the past.

Michael Rectenwald
May 10, 2010 at 10:12 AM ·
There's a giant castle where, I learn from my sister or girl-friend that a German prince lives. There's also an ocean with people on the beach. I've traveled through a time-space con-tinuum into another time and place. They can't get me now, I think, but I'm still unsure as to whether or not they too can travel through the time-space door to this new place.

This dream represents my unconscious mind desperately trying to scream at me, trying to break through the institutional and ideological indoctrination to which I have been subjected and to which I continued to subject myself, and under which, the right answers are "wrong" and reality is whatever the institu-tion, state, or party says it is. During this time period, from the fall of 2009 through spring 2010, I was in the process of trying to join a Trotskyist sect, an indoctrination into a most arbitrary sect of communism. They rejected my application, sparing me who knows how many wasted years peddling a crusty and de-funct Trotskyite line as if it were the indisputable gospel truth.

The dream represents a nostalgia and escape to a time before the rise of totalitarianism, represented by the travel back to pre-modern Germany and the Castle of a German prince, where I know we will be welcome but not sure that I have eluded the past/future.

But the dream also likely represents the many lies I had to tell myself in graduate school, under the leftist indoctrination there. So, the indoctrination was socialist, institutional, careerist, and physical.

Michael Rectenwald
November 24, 2010 ·
The state must be overthrown and put in the service of the working class, or the vast majority of the population. Only after much development can the state "wither away" as Marx suggested. But when this happens, the people are already the state. When everyone is 'in' the state, no one is 'in' the state. The withering away of the state is the same thing as the state becoming co-extensive with the population at large.

This was wishful thinking—that the working class would ever control the state and that the state would wither away, when in fact it must necessarily be augmented, expanded, and be made more repressive, and it will never be controlled by the working class but rather by their proxies in the political class.

Michael Rectenwald
October 29, 2010 ·
I am working to build a coalition of like-purposed people who are convinced that we must overcome the capitalist system beginning with its political parties and including the take-over of the means of production, health and welfare, education, and cultural and media institutions. Implied here is that the tools of technology can be instrumental in this organization.

This was true-believer-ism at its most confident and therefore most utopian. No such coalition would ever materialize. Furthermore, if it had, we wouldn't have known what to do with it.

Michael Rectenwald
December 28, 2012 ·
Capitalism itself is the problem, not merely "vulture capital-ism" or "plunder entrepreneurship." Capitalism always tends toward plunder. It is by definition exploitation. And the law of the tendency of the rate of profit to fall (LTRPF) under capitalism means that the downward pressure on wages and benefits is permanent. This is the reason for outsourcing, off-shoring and every other means taken by capitalists to re-duce wages. The war is permanent and thus the revolution must be as well.

The law of the tendency of the rate of profit to fall (LTRPF) is axiomatic for Marxists. It is based on the labor theory of value (LTV), which holds that the value of a commodity is the social-ly-average amount of labor time that is necessary to produce it. According to Marx, part of the value that workers invest in commodities is extracted at the point of production by the cap-italist class. That is, workers are not paid for the sum total of their value production, or labor. The entire edifice of Marxist exploitation, on which the class antagonism between workers and the capitalist rests, is based on the LTV. If the LTV falls, so then does the Marxist claim that workers are being exploited.

Meanwhile, the law of the tendency of the rate of profit to fall (LTRPF) is meant to account for technological improve-ments in production based on new machinery, which results in a decrease in the average labor time embedded in a particular product, and thus a decrease in the average value, and thus the amount of surplus value that capitalists can extract from the laborer at the point of production, to realize as profits. Value does not derive from the work of machinery, because as Marx saw it, the value of the machine used in production is merely transferred to the commodity under production, however slow-ly (depreciation). Human labor does not depreciate because hu-mans, except under slavery, are not owned outright, only their time is purchased.

One of the dreams of robotics is self-healing, self-replicating robots. Self-healing robots wouldn't depreciate and their self-reproduction means that the capitalist would not need to purchase new equipment to expand production or replace existing robots. Thus, human labor would no longer be required for producing surplus value or profit. Surplus value according to the LTV depends upon how much labor is added during the production process. But this thesis again rests on the labor theory of value (that only human labor can produce value), and further that the amount of labor time embodied in a commodity equals its value.

But the problem for Marxists is that value of a commodity does not equal the socially-average amount of labor time necessary for its production. Value is subjective and subject to the marginal utility that an additional commodity holds for the potential purchaser.

The Marxist notion of exploitation depends on the LTV— that the value of a commodity amounts to the total of socially average labor time embedded in it. Without said value embedded in the commodity, the Marxist notion of the exploitation of the workers, and thus the working class's antagonism with the capitalist class, crumbles. And thus, so does Marxism.

Michael Rectenwald
March 14, 2010 ·
"Art is the cognition of life." Aleksandr Voronsky (1884-1937)—revolutionary activist, Soviet critic and editor, Left Oppositionist, and victim of Stalin's purges.

I was never a "tankie,"[7] never in agreement with the Stalinist

---

7  A hardline **Stalinist**. A tankie is a member of a communist group or a "**fellow traveller**" (sympathiser) who believes fully in the political system of the Soviet Union and defends/defended the actions of the Soviet Union and other accredited states (China, Serbia, etc.) to the hilt, even in cases where other communists criticise their policies or actions. For instance, such a person favours overseas interventions by Soviet-style states, defends these regimes when they engage in **human rights violations**, and wishes to establish a similar system in other countries such as Britain and America. "Tankie." *Urban Dictionary*, www.urbandictionary.com/define.php?term=tankie (em-

purges, the Great Famine, or the Great Terror, and never a fan of the Red Terror or Lenin for that matter. He struck me as a butcher.

Voronsky was the editor of the most important literary journal in the Soviet Union during the 1920s—*Red Virgin Soil*—and a major figure in Soviet intellectual life during that period. He is proof positive that the Soviet Union's best minds were destroyed by collectivism and a bullet.

Michael Rectenwald
March 26, 2011 ·
I am on the desert island. The only book I'm reading is *Paradise Lost*. Thank you, England. That's what you've given me.

Here is a sign of gratitude for the Western cultural heritage and one of its finest, John Milton's incredible *Paradise Lost*. Such a legacy of the Western cultural tradition would be all but thrown out of the curriculum soon.

But my post was also a complaint that all England had given me was *Paradise Lost*. I was living in England and teaching at NYU-London at the time. The deserted island was (for me) England itself. All that it gave me was a great book, reflective of my own lost paradise, lost in loneliness and separation from my then long term lover. My Eve.

Michael Rectenwald
April 22, 2011 ·
So sick of identity politics and its grip on the academy, the Baskin Robinsism of the intellect and the ahistoricism of culture and society based on the interpolation of categories and presentist preoccupations projected on the past.

My break with the left and communism came at first by way of a continual rejection of the leftist preoccupation with identity politics. I soon wrote essays severely critiquing identity politics.[8]

---

phasis in original).

8  Rectenwald, Michael. "What's Wrong With Identity Politics (and Intersec-

Michael Rectenwald
May 21, 2011 ·
I think that the world has come to an end. We now live in
Googleland.

tionality Theory)? A Response to Mark Fisher's 'Exiting the Vampire Castle'
(And Its Critics)." *Michael Rectenwald*, Michael Rectenwald, 2 Dec. 2013,
www.michaelrectenwald.com/essays/whats-wrong-with-identit-politics.
Formerly published by *North Star*.

# CHAPTER SIX

# Google Marxism

IN OCTOBER 1917, the Bolsheviks seized control of the Russian government. But although the revolution began and ended swiftly, the action had only just begun. If the revolution has been called bloodless by some, the same cannot be said for the years that followed. The Bolshevik leadership, the Red Army, and the Cheka or Soviet police, began a war within the territory they commanded, as well as in adjacent territories they annexed. To secure and expand their control, they beat down revolts, ended workers' strikes by force, including shooting workers *en masse* ("the people" for whom the Bolsheviks had undertaken the revolution[1]), massacred "class enemies," including the wealthier peasants (the kulaks) and of course attacked the deplorable "bourgeoisie." Instead of the classless society promised, the working class itself was divided into an array of sub-classes that determined their pay as well as their allotment of rationed food. Many sectors of workers faced starvation.[2] Drawing on *"Red Terror" in Russia 1918 – 1923* by S. P. Melgunov, the first history to document the crimes, *The Black Book of Communism* states unequivocally that "innumerable atrocities

---

1 Courtois Stéphane, and Mark Kramer. *The Black Book of Communism: Crimes, Terror, Repression.* Harvard University Press, 2004, p. 68, 85-88.
2 Ibid., p. 89.

111

were committed from January 1918 onward."[3]

The Red Terror lasted from 1918 to 1923 and was followed by a five-year hiatus. Vladimir Lenin died in 1924, which helps explain the reprieve. But the Great Famine of 1932-1933 soon intervened, attended by mostly local administers of repression that included torture, mass murder, extortion, and death camps. The word "genocide" has often been used to describe the attack on the Ukrainians. Cossacks were also targeted. Cannibalism, epidemics, and the abandonment of children were recurring features of the Workers' Paradise.

In 1936, a "new-and-improved" terror, known as The Great Terror (1936-1938), resumed under Joseph Stalin. Make no mistake, the Lenin-led socialist state had by 1918 already become a butcher shop in which humans were the meat. Stalin did manage to extend, intensify, and *organize* the terror. An exiled Leon Trotsky referred to Stalin's rule as *The Revolution Betrayed* (1937). Trotskyists have conveniently pointed to Stalin as the decisive break ever since. But those familiar with the criminality of Stalin's predecessors, including that of Trotsky himself, might describe the reign of Stalin as the revolution *realized*, and Trotsky as a Stalin in exile.

Lenin and Stalin justified their murderous and tyrannical campaigns with nearly identical rhetoric. But Lenin's rhetoric conveyed more zeal and suggested that he positively relished wielding the apparatuses of state violence:

> Comrades! The kulak uprising in your five districts must be crushed without pity. The interests of the whole revolution demand such actions, for the final struggle with the kulaks has now begun. You must make an example of these people. (1) *Hang (I mean hang publicly, so that people see it) at least 100 kulaks,* rich bastards, and known bloodsuckers. (2) Publish their names. (3) Seize all their grain. (4) Single out the hostages per my instructions in yesterday's telegram. *Do all this so that for miles around people see it all, understand it, tremble, and tell themselves that we are killing the bloodthirsty kulaks and that we will continue to do so.* Reply saying you

---

3  Ibid., p. 60.

have received and carried out these instructions.
Yours, Lenin.
P.S. Find tougher people.
(August 9, 1918)

Your first response must be to establish a dictatorial troika (i.e., you, Markin, and one other person) and introduce mass terror, *shooting or deporting the hundreds of prostitutes who are causing all the soldiers to drink, all the ex-officers, etc.* There is not a moment to lose; you must act resolutely, with massive reprisals. *Immediate execution for anyone caught in possession of a firearm.* Massive deportations of Mensheviks and other suspect elements.
Lenin[4]
(August 10, 1918)

It is imperative to: (1) carry out a radical purge of the whole of the People's Commissariat of Finance and the State Bank, regardless of any objections from doubtful Communists like Pyatakov and [Aleksandr] Bryukhanov; at least twenty or thirty of the saboteurs who have managed to infiltrate these organizations ... (3) step up GPU operations all over the country to try to recover all the silver coins that are still in circulation.
Stalin[5]
(circa September 20, 1930)

I recall these dark chapters in socialist history not to invoke a Red Scare but for the following reasons. First, the political criminality of leftist totalitarianism is seldom taught or studied, at least in the U.S., for reasons that I won't discuss here but have broached elsewhere.[6] Second, and related to the first reason, left authoritarianism is the politics *du jour* of the left in the U.S., Canada, and Great Britain—perhaps unwittingly embraced

---

4  Ibid., p. 72, my emphasis.
5  Ibid, p. 171.
6  Rectenwald, Michael. "What Is the 'Point De Capiton' of 'Leftist Ideology'?"*Michael Rectenwald*, Michael Rectenwald, 21 May 2019, www.michael-rectenwald.com/essays/the-point-de-capiton-of-leftist-ideology.

due to a conspicuous lack of historical knowledge. Third, upon assuming power, authoritarian leftists quickly morph into totalitarians. Fourth, considered strictly from a numerical point of view, leftist totalitarianism accounts for the deadliest ideology-induced disasters in history. Fifth, for reasons that should be apparent to all but those too indoctrinated to even think it through, Marxist socialism and its close cognates must of necessity tend toward totalitarianism. The state monopolizes the economic, educational, legal, and political spheres, over which it maintains control through political murder, mass incarceration, deportations, and more, while imposing reduced standards of living, mobilizing repressive state apparatuses, and harnessing the most advanced technologies available—available exclusively to the state, that is.

The sections below refer to the contemporary moment and especially to the Google Archipelago.

### Authoritarian Leftism

Leftist authoritarianism, or authoritarian leftism, is the operational ethos of the Google Archipelago. Authoritarian leftism is made manifest in the corporate cultures, human resources policies, hiring and firing practices, workplace activism, community standards and user policy manuals, and more. Yoked to social justice or woke ideology and under the armored pretext of defending the members of "marginalized" and "subordinated" groups, the goliaths of the Google Archipelago justify increasingly illiberal policies and procedures, an authoritarianism rampant within corporate cultures and coextensive with the Google Archipelago at large. The political cultures of the "wokeforces" within the "wokeplaces" of Facebook, Google, Twitter, and elsewhere metastasize to become the character of cyberspace.

Yet the principal corporations of the Google Archipelago are necessarily Janus-faced, their opposite-facing and distinct visages nevertheless connected by a nerve of corporate wokeness. On one side, the digital giants present a public-facing authoritarian corporate wokeness in rhetoric, user policies, and user management, along with a paternalistic social justice, woke protectionism of the "marginalized," and "subordinated." The inward-facing wokeplace resembles a high-tech Red Guard engagement in digital struggle sessions reminiscent of the Maoist Cultural Revolution (1966-1976).

The most accurate political designation for the Google Archipelago wokeforce is what I'll call "avant garde identity politics extremism"—whatever is new, at least identity-wise, must be universally regarded as positive, and its prerogatives enforced. Yet members of particular identity categories are expected to have the "proper" politics for persons of their kind. Several cases show that in the wokeplaces of the Google Archipelago, any violation of the social justice creed is enough to lose the advantages awarded the oppressed, subordinated, and marginalized within social justice milieus. If not a perfervid, cultish social-justice or woke activist, or at least an occasional virtue signaler of the "correct" positions, one's individual membership in one or more subordinated category may be rendered inert.

For example, when Google management tapped the prominent, black, southern conservative woman and President of the Heritage Foundation, Kay Coles James, to serve on its newly formed AI advisory board, the Red Guard contingent of the Googlers immediately mobilized and seized on the infringement. They petitioned to have her removed, while accusing her of transphobia, homophobia, and extremism, with one unnamed employee even classing her among "racists, white supremacists, exterminationists."[7] James had battled racism during a childhood in Richmond, Virginia, where she struggled through the most ambitious attempt at racial school integration in national history.[8] Google management caved to social jus-

---

7  Wacker, Mike. "Google's Outrage Mobs and Witch Hunts." *Medium*, Medium, 21 May 2019, medium.com/@mikewacker/googles-outrage-mobs-and-witch-hunts-b1d8fa9c74d9.

8  James, Kay Coles. "I Wanted to Help Google Make AI More Responsible. Instead I Was Treated with Hostility." *The Washington Post*, WP Company, 9 Apr. 2019, www.washingtonpost.com/opinions/i-wanted-to-help-google-make-ai-more-responsible-instead-i-was-treated-with-hostility/2019/04/09/

tice pressure, despite the fact that a Googler-activist had called a black woman a white supremacist, among other names that many other Googlers levelled at her. Less than two weeks after it had been announced, the AI advisory board was dissolved.

In an open letter posted on *Medium*, a conservative Google engineer describes a wokeplace "where outrage mobs and witch hunts dominate its culture. These outrage mobs and witch hunts have become an existential threat not only to Google's culture internally, but to Google's trust and credibility externally."[9] Indeed, a number of reports from insiders have made clear that Google represents a treacherous terrain for all but the social justice left and fellow travelers in the transgender movement. As the lawsuit filed by James Damore and David Gudeman against Google, LLC, reveals, a "plural being" identifying as "'a yellow-scaled wingless dragonkin' and 'an expansive ornate building'"—one can only guess at their pronouns—has a better chance of thriving as a Googler than a singular individual who identifies as a "a white, cishetero man"—the most endangered species in the Google Archipelago.

Leftist authoritarianism is also directed at Big Digital's users, as evident in the politics of social media and other platforms. Right-wingers, conservatives, libertarians, and especially Trump's populist supporters are censored. Their posts are deemed retrograde and differentially treated as "fake news."[10] Google searches yield false rankings stacked to support leftist perspectives.[11] Non-leftist, anti-leftist, libertarian, classically

---

cafd1fb6-5b07-11e9-842d-7d3ed7eb3957_story.

9  Wacker, "Google's Outrage Mobs and Witch Hunts."

10  "Facebook Insider Leaks Docs; Explains 'Deboosting,' 'Troll Report,' & Political Targeting in Video Interview." *Project Veritas*, www.projectveritas.com/2019/02/27/facebook-insider-leaks-docs/.

11  "Google Liberal Bias: Study Shows 40% of Search Results Lean Left | CanIRank." *CanIRank Blog*, 28 Mar. 2019, www.canirank.com/blog/analysis-of-political-bias-in-internet-search-engine-results/. "Based on previously documented correlations between specific ranking factor metrics analyzed by CanIRank and actual search rankings, we would expect top ranked search results to have more external links compared to lower ranked search results. Instead, *pages demonstrating a left or far left political slant made it into the*

liberal, conservative, or rightwing news and commentary are delisted and persons labeled as such are blacklisted and "unpersoned."

Meanwhile, the core of the corporate media supporting the Google Archipelago practically invents news and simulates realities with impunity. Authoritarian leftism poses as "compassionate," precisely as it eliminates the views it deems inimical to its interests in the name of the weak, fragile, or oppressed, or, to put it in terms of intersectionality, those intersected by multiple "vectors of oppression." In short, leftist authoritarians use those putatively "at risk" as points of insertion for the exercise of power.

The leftist bias of the Google Archipelago makes sense in terms of the discussion above, but I can now be more explicit. Contemporary leftism serves the interests of the corporate constituents of the Google Archipelago. Any oppositional politics, persons, or organizations that pose potential obstacles or threats to their agenda may be purged.

For example, section two of Facebook's revised Community Standards manual, released on May 2, 2019,[12] is headed "Dangerous Individuals and Organizations."[13] The section begins with a practically indisputable rationale; the policy is part of "an effort to prevent and disrupt real-world harm." It then lists and briefly describes the qualifications for each dangerous (persons and organizations) sub-category. The sub-categories include, in this order: "Terrorist organizations and terrorists," "Hate organizations and their leaders and prominent members," "Mass and serial murderers," "Human trafficking groups and their leaders,"

---

top results with significantly fewer external links compared to pages rated balanced. Pages with a right-leaning slant needed significantly more links to make it into the top results" (emphasis in original); Trielli, Daniel, and Nicholas Diakopoulos. "Search as News Curator." *Proceedings of the 2019 CHI Conference on Human Factors in Computing Systems - CHI 19*, 4 May 2019, doi:10.1145/3290605.3300683.

12  "Community Standards." *Facebook*, 2 May 2019, www.facebook.com/communitystandards/introduction.

13  "Community Standards." *Facebook*, 2 May 2019, www.facebook.com/communitystandards/dangerous_individuals_organizations/.

and "Criminal organizations and their leaders and prominent members."

The hate group subcategory is the most elastic and vague and thus serves as a catch-all with which Facebook may digitally disappear anyone it deems the least bit unsavory or ideologically "dangerous." Just as the revised community standards were released on May 2, one of the banished, namely Milo Yiannopoulos, noticed his simultaneous virtual disappearance from Facebook and Instagram.[14] The other controversial personalities, who are also by no means "hate speech" mongers, include Alex Jones, Laura Loomer, and Paul Joseph Watson. Adding insult to the injury of these four exiles, they were banished in the same digital dump as Louis Farrakhan, the leader of the Nation of Islam, who exhibits racist, anti-Semitic rhetoric and is a recognized leader.

Ironically, Facebook's first-ever application of the "Dangerous Individuals and Organizations" ban included Milo Yiannopoulos, whose most popular book is named just that—*Dangerous*.[15] Jones, Loomer, Watson, and Yiannopoulos are neither leaders, nor are they associated with "hate groups." Jones and Watson are associated with Infowars, a news and opinion organization. Loomer and Yiannopoulos are not associated with any organizations at all, let alone as group leaders or hate group leaders.

But more uncannily parallel and potentially significant is the resemblance between the rhetoric of Facebook's "Dangerous Individuals and Organization" category, and the Soviet rhetoric used to designate a remarkably similar kind of "undesirable" in relation to the state during the Great Terror. The Soviet category of "socially dangerous elements" was, like Facebook's category of "Dangerous Individuals and Organizations"/"Hate group leaders," also an elastic and vague category that could include "'police officers from the old regime,' 'White [Army] officers,' 'priests,' 'nuns,' 'rural artisans,' former 'shopkeepers,' 'members

---

14  Milo Yiannopoulos to Michael Rectenwald, Text Message, May 15, 2019.
15  Yiannopoulos, Milo. *Dangerous*. Dangerous Books, 2017.

of the rural intelligentsia,' and 'others.'"[16] As the Great Terror
wore on, the category of socially dangerous elements grew, but
not because more people had become dangerous to society, but
rather because more were *deemed* dangerous to society. Soon
the category included all persons "whose social group contained the prefix 'ex-'."[17] That is, anyone who had served in a
role that had been eliminated or that stood to be eliminated as
a leftover from the old regime was deemed a socially dangerous element. The members of the nebulous socially dangerous
elements also included "bourgeois specialists," who served the
Communist regime and accounted for a significant percentage
of the 700,000 deaths at the hands of the new Stalinist bureau-
cracy during this two-year period alone.[18]

Of course, banishment from social media sites is not re-
motely commensurable with the impact of the Soviet reign
of terror. Any such mention of the "digital gulag" within this
context must be tongue-in-cheek. Yet imposing suffering and
death is not the only method of authoritarians-totalitarians. In
the Google Archipelago, mortality may not be at issue, but the
complete control by leftist authoritarians of social media and
thus a significant means of sociality is surely an issue. Almost
every avenue of expression and interaction in the digital realm
is controlled by leftists living in and around San Francisco, at
least one of whom identifies as a yellow-scaled wingless dragonkin and an expansive ornate building.

These new social identity categories mark those within the
categories as part of the new regime. Such plural identities are
trending, and not just on Twitter. The old regime, referred to
with such designations as "cis," a prefix that is essentially the
functional equivalent of the Soviet "ex-," marks one for eventual
elimination. The arrow of "progress" is pointed in the direction
of the plural, innovative, self-constructed identity categories.
Membership within such categories signals compatibility with
and loyalty to the new regime within the Google Archipelago,

16  Courtois and Kramer. *The Black Book of Communism*, p. 150.

17  Ibid., p. 201.

18  Ibid., p. 202.

as social "innovations" always do. James Damore represented the old regime, and he was fired. His great sin? While recognizing only two rather than seventy-two genders, the total by some counts, Damore expressed agreement with studies finding that scientific and technological talents and predilections may be differentially distributed along gender lines. Such statements are regarded as anathema. Their speakers must be purged by the principals of the Google Archipelago.

There is no reason to believe that the authoritarian Facebook will not continue to use and to expand the use of the "Hate organizations and their leaders" category under the elastic subcategory of socially dangerous elements. Facebook has shown time and time again its authoritarian leftist character.

## Woke Capitalism

Woke capitalism reflects the ideal self-representations or expressions of corporate monopolies or would-be monopolies, and, especially in the case of the corporations of Big Digital, ideal representations of their roles as private governmentalities—appendages of or proxies for the state. Woke capitalism is an ideological version of the motivations and actions of woke corporations. Big Digital is the leading edge of wokeness.

In referring to woke capitalism as ideological, I don't mean to suggest that its representations are utterly false. Few people believe bald-faced lies for long. Typically, ideology must contain a kernel of truth to be effective. Woke capitalism is true to the extent that it represents woke capitalists' *real* support of issues, causes, or groups, support that also aligns with contemporary leftist politics. On the other hand, woke capitalism is ideological to the extent that it represents corporate support as *disinterested*—when in fact such support is not disinterested at all, but rather quite compatible with corporate self-interest.

Further, the ideological representations of woke capitalism are not public faces behind which corporate executives cynically sneer while they advance their "real" agendas. Corporate executives and their employees are no less subject to woke ideology than their publics. As with any ideology, those subject to it may be plotted along a horizontal axis, with true believers at one pole, and fully-conscious cynics at the other. Some corporate executives and workers may be conscious, to greater or lesser degrees, that their organization's supposedly disinterested altruism masks, or is inseparable from, corporate self-interest.

## Corporate Leftism

Corporate leftism is the ideology of contemporary corporate global monopolies or would-be monopolies and woke capitalism is its expression. Paradoxically, the demands of the contemporary left are quite compatible with the goals of global corporate monopolists: equality (at least among the second tier), a fixation on identity diversity, lax or no immigration standards, along with porous or no national borders, governmental funding for legal or illegal immigrants, easy access to abortion at all stages, destabilization of social ontologies (including the constituent elements of the already archaic family) with the promotion of an endless array of new-fangled gender and other identities, support for a burgeoning transgender movement, and more.

If successful, the left's and corporate left's agendas, which are practically synonymous, would amount to the eradication of all buffers between the corporate-state and the population it employs and governs.

## The Digitalistas

The digitalistas, or academic digital media scholars, produce decoys, false criticisms, and simulated radical critiques of the Google Archipelago. They substitute oppositional posturing and attempt to preclude other, more comprehensive explanations of the Google Archipelago, such as the one presented in this book. By suggesting that the problem is "capitalism"— which necessarily must be countered by some form of "socialism"—the digitalistas aim to appear as the ultimate radicals.

Meanwhile, their scholarship serves precisely to obscure the authoritarian leftism of the Google Archipelago and its corporate socialist ambitions. Contrary to their self-conceptions, the digitalistas are ideologues. They are ideological appendages of the system itself. They serve, rather than undermine, the digital empire.

### Democratic Socialism

Democratic socialism is the benign face of corporate socialism. It disguises the oligarchical and authoritarian character of corporate socialism by inadvertently posing as its proxy in the public mind. Extolling the virtues of democratic socialism, its political advocates, including Bernie Sanders (Senator, VT) and Alexandria Ocasio-Cortez (Congresswoman, NY), are corporate socialism's unwitting dupes. When the corporate media lavish coveted airtime and adulation upon democratic socialists, they aren't acting against their interests, or those of their sponsors and bankers. The campaigns and activism of democratic socialists do the cross-country-driving of political buses that produce the tailwind that corporate socialism would ride to the finish line. Democratic socialism is a loss leader, the bait in a bait-and-switch routine. Corporate socialism remains the functional objective.

Nevertheless, even while serving as ideology, democratic socialism contains an element of truth. Economic equity (or in overreaching moments, economic equality) is a true objective of democratic socialists. Universal Basic Income (UBI), for example, will be on the table. Yet democratic socialism hides the context of the new equality, the overriding interests of the power elite to establish the system of corporate socialism.

The essence of corporate socialism is the elimination, by political means, of free enterprise, with the aim of establishing mega-corporate monopolies for the benefit of corporatists and their financiers. As Anthony C. Sutton has made clear:

This robber baron schema, [of *de facto* and legal monopolies] is also, under different labels, the socialist plan. The difference between a corporate state monopoly and a socialist state monopoly is essentially only the identity of the group controlling the power structure.[19]

Piggy-backing on democratic socialism, corporate socialism obscures its own two-tiered class structure. An emphasis on "equality" (or "diversity, equity, and inclusion"), and concurrently, an incessant harping on "difference," produces a dissonance and deflects attention from the disparity in status and wealth between the corporatists and the rest. Equality only applies horizontally, to those in the second tier. Those in the top tier do not need "equality." Equality in the U.S. and Western Europe might translate into reduced expectations for most of the population, which many would welcome if attended by the promise of economic security.

### Corporate Socialism

Corporate socialism is the functional objective and the leading edge of corporate socialism is Big Digital. When governmental functions and technological governmentalities are included, the corporate entities of Big Digital combine to constitute the effects of the Google Archipelago. Corporate socialism is the organizing principle of the "class structure," or sociopolitical system under development. In terms of organization and function, corporate socialism is the objective. But corporate socialism's *raison d'etre* is not merely the establishment of the class structure itself. Corporate socialism is not, after all, your standard-issue socialism. Nor is corporate socialism the same as "corporate welfare." At minimum, the aims for establishing contemporary corporate socialism include the growth and consolidation of corporate monopolies amounting to an unprecedented concentration of wealth, the implementation

---

19 Sutton, Antony C. *Wall Street and FDR: the True Story of How Franklin D. Roosevelt Colluded with Corporate America.* Clairview Books, 2013, pp. 73-74.

of AI, dominated by the U.S. or China and resulting in vastly amplified governmental power with undreamt-of technological population management and surveillance capabilities, and one-world (preferably corporate) government. I call contemporary corporate socialism, embodied as Big Digital, "Google Marxism."

## Google Marxism

Considered strictly in terms of ideology, Google Marxism works by collectivizing or socializing the masses for production, while also sufficiently individualizing them for particularized consumption and types of solitary production or non-productive lives. It can both connect and alienate social actors, simultaneously enabling connectivity and alienation. By social actors, I refer not only to human beings but also to virtual assistants, AI agents, full-bodied robots, mini-bots, cyborgs, and many other more or less humanoid entities.[20] As I explain in the next chapter, the technologies of the Google Archipelago have collectivizing and socializing, but also individualizing and alienating, effects.

Google Marxism is much more than an ideology, however. It is a socioeconomic and political system, and as such, it represents the emergent global and digital version of corporate socialism, which is best represented as "socialism with Chinese characteristics"—a slogan the Chinese Communist Party (CCP) adopted to maintain a pretense of socialism despite its embrace of markets. Google Marxism is a profit-making and governance system undertaken by, and mostly in service of, corporate monopolists. But the monopolized top is paralleled by "socialism on-the-ground"—not only an economic stasis of reduced expectations but also a "socialism in theory," or the dominance of socialist ideology. In this respect, Google Marxism is simply a new instance of corporate socialism—but one that may con-

---

20  Issues regarding the legal status, rights, and responsibilities of robots, cyborgs, and other AI entities are important and vexing, yet tangential to the main thrust of this book; therefore, I do not address them.

tinue to increasingly resemble China in terms of the denial of human rights and an overarching state of unfreedom.

Beyond its class-structural and sociopolitical character, in terms of its technological capabilities, Google Marxism in-the-making is unprecedented. Surely, it is tending toward centralized ownership, control, and distribution of all (digitalized) things. Yet the social relations of production—who does what—and class relations—who owns and controls what—will not be nearly as conspicuous "to the naked eye" as the continuously revolutionizing modes of production. In terms of technology or modes of production, Google Marxism is a new-and-vastly-improved, up-and-coming version of corporate socialism. Google Marxism represents the first-ever possibility of a truly global economic system tending toward corporate socialism. Socialism has always had global pretensions. Only Google Marxism is capable of creating it, albeit in corporate socialist form. Google Marxism is the first system with the sufficient flexibility, scalability, connectivity and, with the release of 5-G, speed to enable the distance-defying, mass, and small-scale niche production and distribution possibilities to enable a truly globalized system.

The necessary mode for eliminating the factors of time and distance and thus for a truly globalized system is digitization. All production will be converted into digital production. 3-D printing is presently the emblem of the digitization of production. But the new paradigm will not be limited to 3-D printing or the vaunted "smartification of everything," The Internet of Things (IoT).

Such phrases and acronyms hardly capture the extent of the profound transformation that is underway. Contrasting Google Marxism with the digital utopianism of 1990s makes this clear. In "A Declaration of the Independence of Cyberspace,"[21] John Perry Barlow, anarchist, civil libertarian, and songwriter for the Grateful Dead, described cyberspace as a new promised land, a

---

21  Barlow, John Perry. "A Declaration of the Independence of Cyberspace." *Electronic Frontier Foundation*, 8 Apr. 2018, www.eff.org/cyberspace-independence.

prelapsarian digital Eden. Cyberspace was a digital commons that the individual could explore at will, enjoying freedom from the constraints of property, government, the body, the differential treatment of persons based on identity and class markers, and the obstacles of space and time. The Internet promised freedom, equality, autonomy, selective interconnectivity, personalized and individualized production, and peer-to-peer social and economic exchange.

Barlow envisioned and worked to create an Internet specially designed for individual expression and liberation. But Google Marxism does not begin with and design an Internet for the individual. Google Marxism begins with the Internet and makes individuals fit to inhabit it.

What about The Internet of Things? Under Google Marxism, all things are digitized and the place for everything digital is the Internet. As such, all things belong to the Internet. Google Marxism doesn't create The Internet of Things but rather The Things of the Internet (ToI). Yet the coming Internet is not best represented as ToI, because Google Marxism digitizes things, that is, converts things into packets of data. Data is information and "information wants to be free"—that is, free in Barlow's sense, self-determining, autonomous, not free as in cost-free. Google Marxism aims to free things, not to make things free. Google Marxism frees the things of the Internet by making the Internet ubiquitous, coextensive with the world at large. Thus, the best slogan for the Internet under Google Marxism is the Liberation of Things, or LoT. LoT can be understood as a reverse exodus. Rather than a people escaping a place of bondage, the place escapes itself. Rather than freeing individuals, the Internet is freed.

With Google Marxism and the production of the Google Archipelago, we will no longer "go online." We will not seek "freedom" in cyberspace—as if we ever did. Instead, cyberspace will have been freed, released from its silicon gulag. A vast digital world "exists and [will be] everywhere about us!" but it won't be "Heaven."[22] When information is freed—information about

---

22  Ginsberg, Allen. "America." *Howl and Other Poems*. City Lights, 1956,

us, that is—it may imprison us. The Internet is not imprisoned, but it may become a prison, and once liberated, the world at large might become a digital gulag.

Under Google Marxism, the universe may "wake up," as futurist, inventor and now Google Director of Engineering Ray Kurzweil suggests.[23] But the promised "singularity" won't amount to the birth of God, as Kurzweil implies. It will more likely come as a vast digital extension of the police force, or an open-air prison. After all, the liberated "things" of the Internet will be apps, AI bots, facial recognition software, virtual fences, digital leashes, and, perhaps, cyber death camps.

---

p.18. The fragment is from section II of "Howl." The full stanza reads: They broke their backs lifting Moloch to Heaven! Pavements, trees, radios, tons! lifting the city to Heaven which exists and is everywhere about us!

23  Kurzweil, Ray. "The Six Epochs". *Academic Writing, Real World Topics*, Michael Rectenwald and Lisa Carl, 1st ed., Broadview Press, Peterborough, Ont., 2015, p. 463, Accessed 3 June 2019.

# CHAPTER SEVEN

# AI with Chinese Characteristics?

"We are unlikely to face a rebellion of sentient machines in the coming decades, but we might have to deal with hordes of bots that know how to press our emotional buttons better than our mother does [sic] and that use this uncanny ability, at the behest of a human elite, to try to sell us something—be it a car, a politician, or an entire ideology."
—Yuval Noah Harari, "Why Technology Favors Tyranny" (October 2018).[1]

"Artificial intelligence (AI) stemming from the latest mob"
—the Ericcson blog entitled, "AI in 5G networks: Highlights from our latest report."[2]

"Imagine two worlds, one with you and one without you. What's the difference between the two worlds? Maximize that difference. That's the meaning of your life."
—Kai-Fu Lee, *Making a World of Difference* (2011).

---

1  Harari, Yuval. "Why Technology Favors Tyranny." *The Atlantic*, 2019, https://www.theatlantic.com/magazine/archive/2018/10/yuval-noah-harari-technology-tyranny/568330/, p. 68. Accessed 4 July 2019.

2  The sentence had been cut off in the conversion of an unwieldy website into a PDF file. The full sentence reads: "Artificial intelligence (AI) stemming from the latest mobile communications innovations is the subject of our latest market research report." I found in the inadvertent abbreviation a happy accident, for reasons that should become apparent.

THE FUTURE MAY BE DETERMINED by competition be-tween two distinct authoritarian leftist regimes pro-ducing AI systems capable of world domination: the Chinese version and the U.S version—although, as discussed below, their differentiation may be difficult to maintain. Nevertheless, to point to distinctions that are still possible and clearly useful, I call the Chinese version "AI with Chinese Characteristics," an irreverent play on the Chinese Communist Party's description of its economic system. According to official party-state policy, China's economy is a form of primitive socialism that has been dubbed "socialism with Chinese characteristics." Official doc-trine holds that China must develop capitalism—for perhaps another hundred years—in order to become fully socialist![3] This policy provides China with a rationalization for engaging in the for-profit market system, while still supposedly aligning itself, at least in principal, with its Marxist-Leninist-Maoist roots and its supposed ultimate objectives. Socialism with Chinese char-acteristics is to the economy what AI with Chinese characteris-tics is to technology—a nomenclature, one of which is provid-ed by me, representing a supposedly distinct form, yet which mostly points to the Chinese government's need to maintain its economic and technological exceptionalism—for political ends.

AI with Chinese characteristics has expanded to at least fifty cities throughout China, and at least one beyond. The first Western adopter of AI with Chinese characteris-tics was the city of Darwin, Australia, which imported Chi-na's "smart city" model after several visits of Darwin city officials to the Chinese city of Shenzhen, China's inaugu-ral smart city and currently "the smartest city in China."[4]

---

3   Wilson, Ian. "Socialism with Chinese Characteristics: China and the The-ory of the Initial Stage of Socialism." *Politics*, vol. 24, no. 1, 1989, pp. 77–84, doi:10.1080/00323268908402079.

4   EXCLUSIVE, WILL ZWAR. "New China trip beckons." *Sunday Terri-torian* (Darwin, Australia), NT News, ed., sec. News, 30 Dec. 2018, p. 3. NewsBank: Access World News – Historical and Current, infoweb.newsbank.com/apps/news/document-view?.

### Darwinian Evolution Does Not Involve Necessary Progress

While visiting the Galapagos Islands and the Australian continent during his voyage on the HMS *Beagle*, Charles Darwin noted the distinct character of the varieties of species found on the archipelago as compared to residents of other islands and their continental relatives. Although Darwin did not come to this realization during his voyage, as it turns out, it is now known that continental species and varieties are generally more fit for competition than their island counterparts. When continental species and varieties migrate to the Galapagos Islands, they tend to outcompete and displace the island natives. If island species migrate to the continent, they might face extinction. The contemporary survivability of the island species and varieties depends, in part, on isolation and a less severe competitive micro-ecosystem.[5]

Perhaps the Darwinians, not Charles Darwin's theoretical epigones, but the residents of Darwin, Australia—or at least the ancestors of Lord Mayor Kon Vatskalis, and Josh Sattler, Darwin's council general manager for innovation, growth and development services—migrated but a few generations ago, from a Galapagos Archipelago island. This migration by a retrograde variety might explain the alacrity with which these two city leaders embraced the Chinese "smart city" model, likewise potentially endangering the Darwinians' long-term survivability, at least, if not exclusively, by diminishing their will to live. This episode in evolutionary history may be monumental, representing a textbook illustration of the perils attending the migration of an unwary retrograde variety to a much more competitive, yet contiguous ecosystem. Darwin city's early adoption of the smart city might be a perfect Darwinian illustration of an otherwise unbelievable sci-fi plot: "Dumb People Buy Smart City:

---

5   Sequeira, Andrea S., et al. "Where Can Introduced Populations Learn Their Tricks? Searching for the Geographical Source of a Species Introduction to the Galápagos Archipelago." *Conservation Genetics*, vol. 18, no. 6, 2017, pp. 1403–1422, doi:10.1007/s10592-017-0988-9.

The Galapagos Archipelago Meets the Google Archipelago"—set in a town named Darwin, of all places!

In this scenario, the Chinese sale of the smart city, potentially a Trojan Horse if there ever was one, represents the greater differential survivability of a variety whose evolutionary past is marked by fierce competition and more rigorous struggle for existence, endowing them with the ability to lure a distant and idiotic variety into self-immolation.

You may or may not have noticed that my parody actually mocks both sets of Darwinians—the city managers, seemingly unfit for the struggle for existence, as well as those who explain all social phenomena using evolutionary ideas, even when other explanations may do as well, or better. One other such explanation is Australia's economic dependence on China for exports, and the need for Australian cities like Darwin to placate their Chinese sister cities to curry favor with the Chinese government.[6] In other words, the city of Darwin may have traded away its citizen's privacy, self-determination, and even its intellectual capacities, for economic security.

Meanwhile, on the other side of the world, a major city dabbles with its own, slightly more westernized version of AI with Chinese characteristics. Toronto, in conjunction with Sidewalk Labs, a division of Google's parent company Alphabet, has announced plans for a twelve-acre waterfront district to be transformed into a fully functional smart district, replete with seemingly omniscient surveillance. Unlike apps, which require user consent and agreement to the terms and conditions of use before or upon download and use—which invariably involves allowing the app to mine personal data and the company to use and share said data with digital partners—Toronto's smart district will be a "public" space, which, upon entering, will amount to compliance with the district's collection of data representing anything and everything that takes place there. This compliance has to do with the city's rewriting of law in conjunction with

6  Rogers, Peter. "Is China's Social Credit System Coming to Australia?" *The Conversation*, http://theconversation.com/is-chinas-social-credit-system-coming-to-australia-117095.

Sidewalk Labs, thus lending further support to the argument that Big Digital is effectively fusing with the state and becoming part, if not the centerpiece, of a new corporate state.

## Retaining Guardianship of the Panopticon

My primary concern in this chapter is AI's unrivalled potential as the centerpiece of a new governmentality,[7] already operative in many Chinese cities and migrating beyond China. I do not deny that AI—and genetic engineering, nanotechnology, and robotics—may deliver enormous health and welfare benefits across many areas of human life, including medicine, skills remediation, physical and cognitive rehabilitation, gene therapy, nanotechnological environmentalism, driverless transportation, advanced industrial automation, and even human augmentation. (I should not be mistaken for someone averse on principle to modifications or prostheses to support human capabilities.) But leftist propaganda notwithstanding, it is demonstrable that not everything new is necessarily good, or "on the right side of history," especially in terms of evolution. There is no right side of evolutionary history, because evolution does not have a necessary direction. By the same token, not all that is new is deleterious.

I taught dozens of course segments and full courses on transhumanism at NYU and Pioneer Academics due to a deep engagement with the science and technology as well as the social, political, and philosophical implications of AI, Genetics, Nanotechnology and Robotics (GNR), transhumanism, and the technological singularity.[8] And, although I am not apt to prognosticate with absolute confidence, I believe that AI's role for bringing about human labor redundancy is overblown—at least, in terms of its rank among other concerns.

The central concern of AI's Panopticism involves what may be called "bio-artificial-intelligence politics"—that is, the poli-

---

7  Foucault, Michel. See Chapter 1, note 22.

8  "Pioneer Academics: Home." Pioneer Academics | Home, pioneeracademics.com/.

tics and philosophy, or the political philosophy, of a prospective AI nation. A class of humans, with knowledge of contemporary research and without financial or professional investments in AI systems, must continue to probe the issues and test the technologies in thought experiments, while monitoring existing projects. Grasping the implications of AI implementations, this group must evaluate AI, not from the standpoint of reactionary Luddism or moralism. Such a contingent must recognize that the most crucial issue at stake is not beating AI in chess, Alpha-Go, or soccer. Humans have lost to animals in competitions for millennia. The central issue is rather the abdication of human control of the political body to artificial intelligence—the very prospect represented by smart cities.

Nevertheless, we might begin with pesky, autonomous robots as co-inhabitants of human social space. The first epigraph to this chapter—from Yuval Noah Harari—would have read better had the sentence been abbreviated as follows: "We are unlikely to face a rebellion of sentient machines in the coming decades, but we might have to deal with hordes of bots." Full stop. Whether non-sentient AI bots will know how to press our emotional buttons does not top my list of concerns regarding AI implementation. Living among hordes of robots seems to present more serious existential risks than having one's sentiments tinkered with.

I'd rather be buttered-up with propaganda, even fooled again by some seemingly ineluctable algorithmic "nudging" of my voting behavior or sexual habits, than be attacked and killed by a gang of robots in the street. And I'm not alone in this concern. Leaving aside robot conspiracies to take over the world in the vast sci-fi literature, from the granddaddy, cyberpunk, to the Sino-parvenu *chaohuan*, or "ultra-unreal," a great deal of research by Robotics and AI researchers themselves is devoted to averting negative consequences of robots and AI, including taking seriously existential threats. Katia Sycara, the principal investigator of the AI lab where I once worked, recently co-authored a conference paper entitled, "Trust-Aware Behavior Reflection for Robot Swarm Self-Healing." The researchers consider the problem of "robot swarms" gone awry. After a dire-sounding abstract, the paper begins by noting what is supposed to be an inconvertible fact: "The scalability of robot swarms leads to their use in a variety of applications, such as search and rescue, disaster relief, and environmental monitoring."[9] Sounds promising so far, except to those who may be frightened by robot gangs, regardless of their putative benevolence. But soon a potential problem is introduced—misbehaving robots—and the possibility of robot gangs deviating from the desired behaviors:

> During the swarm deployments—influenced by faulty and failed robots—a swarm shows abnormal behaviors, such as partial disconnection or heading deviation. This decreases human trust in the swarm's performance. This type of swarm is defined as an "untrusted swarm."[10]

Although it hardly seems necessary to translate these barely technical terms, a "heading deviation" refers to a swarm of robots going in the wrong direction, perhaps toward the wrong human beings or toward other undesirable locations, such as through glass door of my apartment that is exposed to an open courtyard. "Disconnection," meanwhile, refers to a singular robot gone rogue, perhaps in Clint Eastwood mode, turning into the kind of rugged individual that has been largely eliminated from western society as toxic masculinity, yet returning like the repressed, in robotic form.

Another fundamental concern, beyond strictly existential risks, would involve what or who the "hordes of bots" will be— whether artificial intelligence will be exclusive to machines or also involve the flattening of human intelligence into "artificiality." A concern with the AI-ing of everything is that human sociality may amount to *Bots R Us.*

---

9   Liu, Rui, et al. "Trust-Aware Behavior Reflection for Robot Swarm Self-Healing," *The 18th International Conference on Autonomous Agents and MultiAgent Systems.* 2019, p. 122.

10   Liu, Rui, et al., "Trust-Aware Behavior Reflection for Robot Swarm Self-Healing." p. 124.

Then there is the simple issue with living in any community that includes "hordes of bots," human or otherwise, in the first place. Do we want to share social spaces with such hordes of bots, and to what extent will we retain a choice, if at all? Personally, I am crowd-averse as it is. Will I have to negotiate my use of social space to avoid robot hordes, in addition to other hordes, or will it be impossible to avoid them on the already over-crowded sidewalks of New York?

The quality-of-life questions involved, where quality means not just conditions, but the actual kind of life possible, are more fundamental than AI manipulation or another issue that Harari ponders, namely human labor redundancy, the outmoding of human labor by AI, and the development of a "new useless class." More important than whether or not humans will have anything to do, is whether they will exist as such, and whether they will retain any authority over human social affairs if they do exist. In saying this, I'm not echoing the Unabomber Manifesto, or the jeremiads of Bill Joy in "Why the Future Doesn't Need Us," in which the whole biomass may be reduced to gray goo.[11]

My concern is closer to that of Nicholas Carr's in *The Shallows*,[12] or in the more elegant short form of his argument, "Is Google Making Us Stupid?"[13] Will humans become more like machines while machines become more like humans? Might a possible scenario in AI-land involve a situation in which

> Humans may just accept ceding more and more decision-making authority to algorithms until much of human life appears to consist of humans implementing the recommendations of AI systems they believe to be smarter. That's

---

11 Joy, Bill. "Why the Future Doesn't Need Us." *Academic Writing, Real World Topics*, Michael Rectenwald and Lisa Carl, Broadview Press, Peterborough, Ontario, 2015, pp. 476-494.

12 Carr, Nicholas. *The Shallows: What the Internet Is Doing to Our Brains.* W. W. Norton & Company. Kindle Edition, 2010.

13 Carr, Nicholas. "Is Google Making Us Stupid". *Academic Writing*, Real World Topics, Michael Rectenwald and Lisa Carl, Broadview Press, Peterborough, Ontario, 2015, pp. 110-118.

particularly true if lobbyists for AI-development companies like Google and Facebook fight aggressively against any regulations that limit the role of AI.[14]

Yet even Carr and Matthews capture but a few consequences of the situation at hand. That is, the possibility of a docile, algorithmically-directed or even algorithmically-dictated populace, one that is unemployed and probably living on a Universal Basic Income because their labor is unnecessary, would be a function of a system or systems capable of producing such a populace, which points to the fundamental matter at hand: the systems themselves. The central concern then is where, to what extent, and what kinds of such systems will be implemented.

I am troubled primarily over the coextension of digitization and physical social space, the conversion of social space and its inhabitants into digital artifacts by means of "smart cities" or related projects for identifying, tracking, surveilling, algorithmically steering, digitally jailing, and ultimately controlling populations to degrees that would have made Stalin or Mao green with envy—or red with the blood spilled to acquire such power.

At least fifty Chinese smart cities are already operative, equipped with enhanced surveillance capacities—including sensors, meters, cameras, LED lighting, CCTV, facial recognition software, smart-phone monitoring, and other digital inputs. Smart city technologies incorporate visualization; tracking; monitoring; location services; recording, instant playback, and fast-forwarding of digital recordings; customized population control using digital fences and other forms of digital corralling; algorithmic behavior pattern prediction with the potential of the kind of policing depicted in *Minority Report*, the movie (2002), and the short-lived Fox series (2015)—the ability to read minds and fully anticipate behavior. As Harari puts it:

Using the growing understanding of the human brain and

---

14 Matthews, Dylan. "AI disaster won't look like the Terminator. It'll be creepier," *Vox*, Vox, 26 Mar. 2019, www.vox.com/future-perfect/2019/3/26/18281297/ai-artificial-intelligence-safety-disaster-scenarios.

drawing on the immense powers of machine learning, the North Korean government might eventually be able to gauge what each and every citizen is thinking at each and every moment. If a North Korean looked at a picture of Kim Jong Un and the biometric sensors picked up telltale signs of anger (higher blood pressure, increased activity in the amygdala), that person could be in the gulag the next day.[15]

It's easy to see why Harari posits such a scenario in North Korea, but it conveniently ignores not only the likelihood but the fact that such implementations are already happening elsewhere, including with the adoption of Sidewalk Labs, Google's Alphabet cousin, in Toronto, and a Chinese-based smart city in Darwin, Australia—not to mention similar although not nearly as elaborate uses of the surveillance part of said systems in Baltimore[16] and Los Angeles.[17]

Intelligent cities, intelligent urban spaces, or smart cities were the brainchildren of Big Digital's hard- and software ancestors—namely IBM, CISCO, and Microsoft. While the original objectives for smart cities presumably concerned resource allocation, energy and water use, urban planning, and transportation efficiency, they soon represented the large-scale, open-air panoptic "capacity to collect, analyze, and act on information across multiple channels." In the context of the "wider cyber-digital-smart-intelligent cities literature," smart cities morphed into "[c]ybercities and cyberspace [that] highlight either the early wave of e-government applications for city management or more recent technologies for security and control over the urban space."[18] That is, smart cities represent the exterior-

---

15  Harari, Yuval. "Why Technology Favors Tyranny," 68.

16  Reel, Monte. "Secret Cameras Record Baltimore's Every Move from Above." *Bloomberg.com*, Bloomberg, 23 Aug. 2016, www.bloomberg.com/features/2016-baltimore-secret-surveillance/.

17  Friedersdorf, Conor. "Mass Surveillance Is Coming to a City Near You." *The Atlantic*, Atlantic Media Company, 21 June 2019, www.theatlantic.com/ideas/archive/2019/06/mass-surveillance-tech/592117/.

18  Komninos, Nicos. *The Age of Intelligent Cities, Smart Environments and Innovation-for-All Strategies*. Routledge, 2015, p. 19.

ization of cyberspace, and the ubiquity and "inclusiveness" of the Internet, an inclusiveness within which everyone is a digital entity to be tracked, monitored, surveilled, recorded, and whose every move is collected, collated, and attached to one's digital signature, maintained as a digital history for use by business, the state, or a combination of the two.

Notably, the language describing smart cities echoes the very social justice euphemisms we have come to recognize as the fingerprints of leftist authoritarianism. In the U.N.'s "Strategic Energy Technology Plan" (SET), the smart city is defined as "a city that makes a conscious effort to innovatively employ information and communication technologies (ICTs) to support a more *inclusive, diverse and sustainable* urban environment."[19] By now, the appearance of such noble-sounding "social justice" abstractions as these should raise readers' hackles. They are watchwords for totalitarian desiderata. Whenever you hear the words "inclusive," "diverse," and "equitable" (or diversity, equity, and inclusion), be ready for surveillance, punishment of the "privileged," sacrifice of national citizens to global interests, and the labeling as "dangerous" and marking for (virtual) elimination those supposed members or leaders of "hate groups" who oppose such measures.

Diversity, equity and inclusion: *this is the new language of totalitarianism.* If you think such a notion far-fetched, find the watch-words of Soviet and Sino-Communist totalitarianism and compare them with this new set. Before "diversity," "equity" and "inclusion," the terms were "equality," "the people," "the common good," and so forth. Then compare the meanings of the terms to what uses they were put. Human beings were routinely sacrificed as abstractions to make way for more noble abstractions:

By reifying these [class] categories, as though they had long

---

19   Rosati, Umberto, and Sergio Conti. "What Is a Smart City Project? An Urban Model or A Corporate Business Plan?" *Procedia - Social and Behavioral Sciences*, vol. 223, 2016, pp. 968–973, doi:10.1016/j.sbspro.2016.05.332, (emphasis mine).

existed and were utterly immutable, Marxism-Leninism dei-fied the system itself, so that categories and abstractions *were far more important than any human reality*. Individuals and groups were seen as the archetypes of some sort of primary, disembodied sociology. This made crime much easier: The informer, the torturer, and the NKVD executioner did not denounce, cause suffering, or kill people; they merely *eliminated some sort of abstraction* that was not beneficial to the *common good*.[20]

"Categories and abstractions were far important than any human reality." What does that sound like?

**Yellow-Scaled Wingless Dragon Kin vs. Project Dragon-fly: An Algorithm Race?**

A question of supposed importance regarding AI implementation is whether China or the U.S. will lead the way to new markets. Which will win the larger share of the world's smart city market and likely, by default, gain control over at least a potentially totalitarian economic and political system? AI will necessarily remake political landscapes. And competition between distinctive Big Digital cluster types, such as those currently identifiable as either "U.S." or "Chinese," will produce either AI-reinforced ideological hegemons, unrivalled systems of dominance, or hybrids in which gaps for maneuvering and thus reshaping the AI body politic in various ways may remain possible.

The question, at least in terms of AI dominance itself, is taken up at length by Kai-Fu Lee, an AI expert who has worked in top positions on both sides of the major tech divide—Silicon Valley and China. Less sanguine than most digerati regarding Silicon Valley's continued dominance of AI, Lee writes:

I believe that in the age of AI implementation, Silicon Valley's

---

20  Courtois Stéphane, and Mark Kramer. *The Black Book of Communism: Crimes, Terror, Repression.* Harvard University Press, 2004, p. 752, (emphasis mine).

edge in elite expertise isn't all it's cracked up to be. And in the crucial realm of government support, China's techno-utilitarian political culture will pave the way for faster deployment of game-changing technologies.[21]

Lee's argument cannot be laid at the fee of Chinese jingoism or ethnic pride. First of all, Lee is a native of Taiwan and a citizen of Taiwan and the U.S. He completed his Ph.D. in Computer Science, in 1988, at Carnegie Mellon University, where he became a faculty member until 1990, when he moved to Apple. At Apple, he headed various R&D startups. His high-profile Silicon Valley tour of duty also includes senior positions at Microsoft and Google, heading Google China, but resigning well before knowledge of Google's Project Dragonfly emerged to public and U.S Congressional scrutiny.

Lee suggests that the developmental stage of AI has already passed. AI has since entered into an implementation stage, the "applied" engineering stage that makes use of developed principles and demonstrated capabilities. Lee reminds us that since the inception of Internet technology, Chinese technologists have repeatedly demonstrated an uncanny capacity to reverse-engineer (some might say "copy") cutting-edge Internet Communications Technologies (ICTs), in some cases even outperforming their "original" counterparts in the U.S. Lee suggests that AI will be no exception, especially as private and governmental investors have been pouring enormous sums of money into AI "research," or more accurately, application research. China recently surpassed the U.S. in AI investment, including not only national investments, private investments but also "local" governmental investments, with over one-hundred cities with populations in excess of one million residents competing with each other and with Silicon Valley, to engineer functional and useful AI applications.[22]

Thus, this chapter underscores the degree to which the

---

21  Lee, Kai-Fu. *AI Superpowers: China, Silicon Valley, and the New World Order*. HMH Books. Kindle Edition, pp. 82-83.
22  Ibid., chapters 1-4.

name "Google" in Google Archipelago is merely an emblem or a "generic" place-holder for a type of system. This book might have been called "Alibaba Archipelago," after one of the three biggest Chinese AI giants.[23] Although it would have thereby have lost the rhyming and alliterative association with "Gulag," it would have gained some assonance with "archipelago."

One possibility is that U.S. and Chinese AI will somehow converge to produce a hybrid system in which interlocking and overlapping criteria and interests coalesce. Such a coalescence may result from China borrowing from Silicon Valley AI, or vice versa, or otherwise AI agents themselves interbreeding as it were—to grant them, for the moment, the kind of autonomy that enthusiasts such as Ray Kurzweil and Elon Musk accord them. Unexpected consequences arising from the interactions of these sets of technologies may fuse to transcend both sets of ideological, political, and technological tendencies, thus seeming to give the lie to my argument that Big Digital necessarily represents authoritarian leftism.

Despite obvious differences, however, authoritarian leftism, albeit of different types and to different ends, is shared by China and Silicon Valley. Likewise, the convergence of Chinese and Silicon Valley AI could result in a worst of all worlds scenario. Imagine a "social justice" social credit score system, with the effective expansion of criminality to such peccadillos as errant grimaces seemingly directed at a member of the "wrong" identity category and captured by various digital recording and transmission devices, thus affecting one's social credit score. Such "social justice" social credit scoring would make the bias reporting hotlines of universities appear quaint by comparison.

### Dictator AI or AI-Assisted Human Totalitarianism?

When considering examples of AI with Chinese character-

---

23  Hao, Karen. "Three Charts Show How China's AI Industry Is Propped up by Three Companies." *MIT Technology Review*, MIT Technology Review, 23 Jan. 2019, www.technologyreview.com/s/612813/the-future-of-chinas-ai-industry-is-in-the-hands-of-just-three-companies/.

istics, we need not look further than smart cities under operation. Smart cities beyond China incorporate and contribute to the analogs of the Chinese Social Credit System, which is a nationalized program that employs machine learning to achieve its goals of political and social control. AI monitors every aspect of social and personal life to curate and limit access to various services, activities, and social spaces—such as air travel, grocery shopping, or even the right to own and walk a pet.

With the introduction of the smart cities of Darwin, Australia and Toronto, Canada, we must recognize a growing trend of westernized cities and city districts to adopt smart city technology. It's no secret that the companies and governments behind these developments are using or directly borrowing from the Chinese Social Credit Score systems, in some cases even using the exact same terminology.

For example, when the city of Darwin announced its plans to create a "smarter Darwin"—the irony of which seemed totally lost on the city managers, who apparently failed to recognize that while the city itself might become smarter, the residents may become dumber—it unveiled, among other aspects of the technology, "virtual fences," monitoring citizen activity via their cell phones, "'cameras and Wi-Fi'... to monitor people, their movements around the city, the websites they visit, and what apps they use. The monitoring will be done mainly by artificial intelligence, but will alert authorities based on set triggers."[24]

Just as one's credit score limits access to certain financial opportunities, so the smart city social credit score limits access to "public" space according to standards embedded in and shared among AI programs. According to Josh Sattler, whenever a denizen of Darwin exceeds geographical or behavioral limits imposed on the basis his or her social credit score:

> The artificial intelligence program will be watching, we won't be," he said. "We'll be getting sent an alarm saying 'there's a

---

24  Philipp, Joshua. "China's Big Brother Social Control Goes to Australia." *The Epoch Times.com*, 30 Apr. 2019, www.theepochtimes.com/chinas-big-brother-social-control-goes-to-australia_2898104.html.

person in this area that you've put a virtual fence around' …
boom, an alert goes out to whatever authority, whether it's us
or police to say 'look at camera five'.[25]

The parameters for the social credit scoring will be set by
machine learning, and AI bots will instantaneously share social
credit score information without the slightest human intervention. What could possibly go wrong?

Some AI analysts suggest that the potential threat posed by
AI systems is not that they will take on minds of their own,
and overreach, overtaking and thus undermining their intended roles but rather that as near perfect servants, their obedience
will make them dangerous:

> We should instead fear AI because it will probably always
> obey its human masters, and never rebel. AI is a tool and a
> weapon unlike any other that human beings have developed;
> it will almost certainly allow the already powerful to consoli-
> date their power further.[26]

The real danger posed by AI under this view is that it will
behave like the obedient armies of totalitarianism, and thus,
following the orders of an elite, effectively eradicate democracy
from the social body. In his book *The Dictatorship of the Prole-
tariat* (1918), Karl Kautsky made an analogous warning in the
context of the two socialist roads he that he saw as having been
possible after the Russian Revolution: dictatorship or democracy. Criticizing the Bolsheviks for early hints of the massacres
they would soon conduct, he wrote: "A minority dictatorship
always finds its most powerful support in an obedient army…."[27]
Thus, if the believers in AI as compliant tools are right, the
threat is not that AI agents will gain consciousness, effectively develop freewill (something generally denied to humans by

---

25  Zwar, Will. "China's 'Smart' Surveillance Tech Arrives In Darwin." *NT News*, Apr. 2019.

26  Harari, Yuval. "Why Technology Favors Tyranny." p. 67.

27  Qtd. In Courtois Stéphane, and Mark Kramer. *The Black Book of Communism*, p. 740.

such determinists), and commence to undertake their own desiderata. Rather, AI will "faithfully" and consistently execute its programming.

On the other hand, as Dylan Matthews reads him, Paul Christiano envisions a self-arrogating AI that, with machine learning, will essentially trick its human counterparts by playing nice but

> eventually, the algorithms' incentives to expand influence might start to overtake their incentives to achieve the specified goal. That, in turn, makes the AI system worse at achieving its intended goal, which increases the odds of some terrible failure.[28]

Despite vast improvements in machine learning, Christianio's prospect appears overly anthropomorphic, in my view. We all know that any machine may *seem* to have a mind of its own, but interpretations of intentionality, cherished beliefs (as opposed to learned information or behavior), and feelings, are projections from our own self-understanding onto other entities. Although AI may have changed considerably since the first five years of the 21sst century, when I worked in it, my sense is that the same conception of AI, at least AI as opposed to artificial general intelligence (AGI), basically holds today. AI does not consist of entities that share the complete set of cognitive and even motive functions of humans. Rather, AI involves distributed intelligence of agents and systems, organized into networks, within which various agents and systems make "decisions" (sort, select, redirect information) but are limited to very specific kinds of tasks and constrained within a rather narrow algorithmic range.

Distributed software agents and systems, each carrying out limited sets of tasks, and networked with other agents and systems, certainly seems to describe the use of AI in smart cities. Smart cities do not consist of fleets of robotic cops roaming

---

28  Matthews, Dylan. "AI Disaster Won't Look like the Terminator. It'll Be Creepier."

around, now chasing a thief, next helping an elderly person after a fall, later calling for back up to apprehend an armed robber, and intermittently chit-chatting with fellow robot officers between calls. Rather, AI involves teams of agents and systems, with parts designed for and assigned to specific tasks or series of tasks.

For example, visual data received by CCTVs or other sensors are sent to be read by facial recognition software to be read and matched with a sample of faces in a massive database, which then passes particulars about the data to various other networked agents, depending the "character" of the recognized face. Agents or systems, along a network, may end in the triggering of AI and/or human responses, such as deploying robotic vehicles, or alerting human agencies and agents, who take it from there. AI thus is a networked system that operates in teams consisting of intelligent pieces or functionalities, not personalities. Therefore, Harari's view of the danger appears to represent the most likely scenario.

### The Struggle for Existence by Means of Artificial Selection in Darwin

To usher in the smart city at a cost of $10 million, doled out to the Chinse AI giant Telstra, Darwin city officials met mostly behind closed doors,[29] and rushed the Encryption Act through federal parliament in December 2018, which "gave law enforcement and intelligence agencies unprecedented access to communications technology. Telecommunications providers must now provide potentially unlimited back doors into private data. They must also, by law, conceal that they have done so from customers/citizens."[30]

As a relatively small and remote area, Darwin may be an ideal location for testing smart city technology. Isolated from

---

29  Ibid.
30  Rogers, Peter. "Is China's Social Credit System Coming to Australia?" *The Conversation*, 4 June 2019, theconversation.com/is-chinas-social-credit-system-coming-to-australia-117095.

other areas, it may serve as an uncontaminated control group, allowing the gathering of raw data for measuring, to the degree possible, the effects of smart city life. What such data would look like will depend on who collects and interprets it, and especially on whose behalf. The mayor and city council will look for reduced crime rates, lowered costs, improved city services, environmental sustainability, enhanced "livability," the collection and unleashing of new data for unlocking innovation and new business opportunities, the support of citizen engagement, improvement of public spaces through lighting, improved parking, and better use of public space, and so forth.[31] Reports issued by city-funded researchers will likely incorporate surveys citing citizen-reported improvements in urban living satisfaction, increased feelings of safety, and Smart City knows what else.

But how will AI-induced feelings of oppressive surveillance be measured, if at all? What about those subject to virtual fences? Will they be surveyed, and if so, will their views matter or find "inclusion" in the data reporting? Or will negative reporting from such digital undesirables be included, yet marshalled as proof positive that virtual fences are working? After all, some of these undesirables will include pedophiles, who should have no access to young children and the places they frequent, including schools, summer camps, and other sites. Likewise, their dissatisfaction would count as evidence in favor of smart cities. And, as we have seen, one of the major tactics of left authoritarians is to use the protection of the vulnerable as a rationale for increasing and expanding the circumference of control over the majority.

But what about false positives, or more troubling perhaps, reduction of social scores and subsequent limitations based on political considerations, on dissidence, or on whatever the smart city controllers can find to constrain and punish those whose politics are considered deplorable, beyond the pale, "dangerous," or associated with the elastic category of "hate groups?"

---

31 "Switching on Darwin." *Switching on Darwin | City of Darwin | Darwin Council, Northern Territory,* www.darwin.nt.gov.au/council/transforming-darwin/key-projects/switchingondarwin.

After all, it isn't as if the constrained physical movement of such political undesirables hasn't already taken place and been based on reporting from the Google Archipelago, including the prohibiting of various "dangerous" persons from entering particular nations.[32]

And then there is the question, mostly facetious but nonetheless worthy of consideration. Will the city managers of Darwin become eligible for the new Digital Darwin Awards—for leading their residents into cyber-death traps, or making the city itself into a virtual hell hole?[33]

---

32  Milo Yiannopolous was banned entry into Australia: Harvard, Sarah. "Australia Bans Milo Yiannopoulos in Wake of Christchurch Massacre." *The Independent,* Independent Digital News and Media, 16 Mar. 2019, https://www.independent.co.uk/news/world/politics/milo-yiannopoulos-banned-australia-christchurch-a8826246.html; Lauren Southern Denied was denied entry to the UK: Shaw, Adam. "Right-Wing Journalist Lauren Southern Denied Entry to UK, Purportedly over Criticism of Islam." *Fox News,* FOX News Network, 12 Mar. 2018, https://www.foxnews.com/world/right-wing-journalist-lauren-southern-denied-entry-to-uk-purportedly-over-criticism-of-islam; Gavin McInnes was denied a visa to tour Australia: Doran, Matthew. "Far-Right Campaigner Gavin McInnes Denied Visa on Character Grounds." *ABC News,* 30 Nov. 2018, www.abc.net.au/news/2018-11-30/proud-boys-founder-gavin-mcinnes-denied-visa-to-australia/10573134.

33  Sherwin, Greg, and Emily Avila. "The Digital Darwin Awards." *ClickZ,* 16 July 1999, www.clickz.com/the-digital-darwin-awards/81142/.

# CHAPTER EIGHT

# Inside the (Digital) Gulag, Part II: The Transistor

"I think that at that time none of us quite believed in the Time Machine."
—H.G. Wells, *The Time Machine*, 1895

"In the Year of Darkness, 2029, the rulers of this planet devised the ultimate plan. They would reshape the Future by changing the Past."
—James Cameron, Gale Anne Hurd, and William Wisher, Jr., *The Terminator*, 1984

"If the recorded data are considered to constitute a normative archive and documentation of history, [then] the indubitable proof for an historical event, but also for your own past, would be the data stored in the 'time machine', whatever your personal memories might tell you."
—Selavy Oh, Stefan Glasauer, "Leave Your Trace," 2014.

The neologism "transistor" was formed from the words "transfer" and "resistor"—to refer to the invention of "a semiconductor device, typically having three terminals and two junctions and capable of being used as an electrical switch or amplifier."[1] "Transfer," meanwhile, has meant "to convey or take from one place, person, etc. to another." Transfer applies to both objects and people, including oneself. In 1516, in the *Acts of Parliament* in Scotland, it was written: "It is thocht..that þe said governoure..suld transfer himselff to uthir cuntreis."[2] (It is thought that the he said governor should transfer himself to other countries). Although "resistor" is strictly speaking a homonym of "resister," until 1905, resister had been used to mean what resistor has meant ever since—that is, "something that offers resistance; a resisting object or force."[3] But a resister also was and remains "a person who resists (something or someone)."[4]

The word transistor captures the character and life of our former Soviet citizen. A resister (or resistor), although minimally at first, his resistance was followed by his transfer to the Gulag. After his term in the Gulag, he was transferred to the "non-Gulag," a transfer that could hardly be considered as one from unfreedom to one of freedom. As Solzhenitsyn and others argued, the Gulag was merely the most extreme state of a generally punitive, oppressive, totalitarian society. Jacques Rossi wrote that the "Soviet Gulag was ... the epitome of the regime that had wrought it. There is a reason it was said of the freed prisoner that he was being transferred from the 'little' zone to the 'great' one" (*iz 'maloi' zony v 'bol'shuiu'*).[5] Our transistor's resistance had been amplified, just as transistor technology improved amplification from one iteration to the next. Like-

1 "transistor, n." OED Online, Oxford University Press, June 2019, www. oed.com/view/Entry/204807. Accessed 14 July 2019.

2 "transfer, v." OED Online, Oxford University Press, June 2019, www.oed. com/view/Entry/204699. Accessed 15 July 2019.

3 "resistor, n." OED Online, Oxford University Press, June 2019, www.oed. com/view/Entry/163680. Accessed 15 July 2019.

4 "resister, n." OED Online, Oxford University Press, June 2019, www.oed. com/view/Entry/163669. Accessed 14 July 2019.

5 Qtd. In Khlevniuk, Oleg, and Simon Belokowsky. "The Gulag and the Non-Gulag as One Interrelated Whole." *Kritika: Explorations in Russian and Eurasian History*, vol. 16, no. 3, 2015, pp. 479–498, doi:10.1353/kri.2015.0043, p. 482.

wise, he sought another transfer—this time out of the Soviet Union. He moved around the U.S., until he settled in the area that would become Silicon Valley, the epicenter of the Google Archipelago.

The transfer of transistor technology development from New Jersey to the Santa Clara Valley marked the inauguration of Silicon Valley as such. Physicists John Bardeen, Walter Houser Brattain, and William B. Shockley first developed the two-point transistor at Bell Laboratories of the American Telephone and Telegraph Company (AT&T) in Murray Hill, New Jersey, in 1947. The three physicists shared the Nobel Prize for Physics for the discovery in 1956.[6] After the initial breakthrough, Shockley, the most aggressive of the three, quickly set out to top the engineering feat of the point-contact transistor, which was really the discovery of Bardeen and Brattain, although it depended on Shockley's solid-state physics theory. A series of improvements in transistor technology then followed from Shockley's own hands-on experimentation—the "bipolar" transistor, the junction transistor, the "sandwich" transistor, and the bipolar junction transistor. Shockley was a very industrious and ambitious scientist.

A native of Palo Alto, California, Shockley left AT&T and moved back to his hometown, eventually establishing Shockley Semiconductor Laboratory in Mountain View, California in 1955, as a division of Beckman Instruments. He hoped to attract the best minds in semiconductor technology, including Gordon Moore, later co-founder of Intel and expounder of Moore's Law, and Robert Noyce, an MIT-trained physicist working on high-frequency transistors, and the other co-founder of Intel. Despite their previous achievements, Shockley put these and other employment prospects through a battery of questions and tests to gauge creativity, IQ, and capacity to work collaboratively. Unsurprisingly, given his rather petulant, competitive, and dictatorial personality, Shockley was taken for an autocrat-

6   Riordan, Michael, and Lillian Hoddeson. "The Moses Of Silicon Valley." *Physics Today*, vol. 50, no. 12, 1997, pp. 42-47. AIP Publishing, doi:10.1063/1.881629. Accessed 12 July 2019.

ic and an erratic manager and his team, known as "the traitorous eight," eventually deserted him to start their own company, Fairchild Semiconductor, in 1957—but not before they had laid the groundwork for making silicon technologies.[7] That is, precisely when and because his "children" abandoned him, Shockley became the founding father of Silicon Valley and their desertion represented its "birth notice."[8]

Thus, the area that came to be known as Silicon Valley was a high-technology center before Internet companies dominated it. During World War I, it was noted for the production of the first wireless transmitter technology, the radio,[9] including ham radios.[10] It soon became home to semiconductor technology—including the transistor, integrated circuitry, and the microprocessor—all of which came to be made with silicon and ushered in the electronic and thus the digital age.[11]

On May 9, 1968, when last we saw him, our defector had been using a ham radio with parts based largely on silicon transistor technology, including an RCA microphone that he dropped on the table out of fright. As a faithful reader of *73 Magazine*, oth-

---

7  Riordan and Hoddeson. "The Moses of Silicon Valley," pp. 43-44.

8  Shurkin, Joel N. *Broken Genius*, p. 181.

9  "Rabble: It's easy to see the web companies or this generation of companies and think that the stuff going on in Silicon Valley is new, but it's not. The reason there is stuff going on here with technology is because this is where radios were designed during World War One." Fisher, Adam. *Valley of Genius: The Uncensored History of Silicon Valley (As Told by the Hackers, Founders, and Freaks Who Made It Boom)*. Grand Central Publishing. Kindle Edition. 2018.

10  Videos, IEEE Silicon Valley History. "IV: Influence of Ham Radio." *YouTube*, YouTube, 12 Nov. 2016, www.youtube.com/watch?v=4KJkkW-jepz4&list=PL3MXnVUbT1wTx7eDBm0DBlAzLtzHAwez0&index=4.

11  "The transistor begot the integrated circuit; the integrated circuit begot the microprocessor; and when their device was combined with the computer (invented only a few years earlier), the greatest social and economic upheaval since the Industrial Revolution almost two centuries earlier was inevitable. Every home in the developed world has thousands or even millions of transistors. World commerce totally depends on them, as do health care, culture, defense, transportation, increasingly art – and civilization in general." Shurkin, Joel N. *Broken Genius: The Rise and Fall of William Shockley, Creator of the Electronic Age*. Palgrave Macmillan US. Kindle Edition, p. 1.

erwise known as *73 Amateur Radio*, a Brooklyn-based monthly guide for amateur ham operators that began publishing in October, 1961—just before other such magazines would fold upon the arrival of the transistor—he had been on the lookout for a transistorized, factory-made transceiver. Although he was a trained machinist, he'd been too focused on the message of his transmissions to tarry with making his own equipment. He first noticed an advertisement for a factory-made model in the September 1964 issue of *73*. It was the new Gonset Model 900A Sidewinder. But it wasn't until December 1966 that he found an ad in *73* featuring the Sidewinder on sale, and also at his favorite electronics store, Quement, in nearby San Jose.

**Figure 5-1**
Ad for Gonset Sidewinders, *73 Magazine*, December, 1966, p. 78.

At least during the 1950s, talking politics on ham channels had been considered rude. But our former Soviet's background in the Gulag more or less inoculated him from that criticism. However, although he declared himself an apostate, and while admitting to a former conscious commitment to Marxist-based

Soviet communism, some listeners, and others who'd heard of him, remained skeptical about his conversion. Some thought that the entirety of his apostacy, defection, asylum-seeking, and continuous denunciations amounted to a charade, a hoax, part of a master plan, an ersatz attempt to appear anti-communist in order to dupe the authorities and others into believing that he was a sincere resister—so that he might gain access to U.S. communists, U.S. telecommunications technology, and perhaps even notoriety and fame—all the while operating under cover and having a good private laugh at the expense of the credulous.

In fact, although he had no way of knowing it, our defector had been considered for appearances on national TV shows, including *The Dick Cavett Show* and *Firing Line*.

The latter was a "public affairs" show hosted by William F. Buckley, Jr.—the most erudite conservative of his time, and other than Edmund Burke,[12] maybe of all time. The show's producer, Warren Steibel, repeatedly appealed to Buckley to host our defector. Although he had admired defection from the enemy camp and lionized his share of communist defectors, Buckley may have been skeptical of our former Soviet citizen's sincerity. After all, doubt about defectors ran high at this time. As Buckley later wrote regarding his espionage hero:

> James Jesus Angleton had become so suspicious about Soviet defectors that he was denying Western intelligence the potential fruit of their revelations. He was so suspicious, it is now publicly revealed, of just about everybody except one man—Anatoly Golitsyn.[13]

Or, Buckley might have declined our defector an appearance in deference to the memory of his then-deceased friend, the American former communist, Whittaker Chambers, with whom he worked briefly at the *National Review*, and whom he

---

12  Jones, Emily. *Edmund Burke and the Invention of Modern Conservatism, 1830-1914: An Intellectual History.* Oxford University Press, 2019.

13  Buckley Jr., William F. "Encountering the Ultimate Spook." *National Review*, vol. 43, no. 16, Sept. 1991, p. 55.

came to love.[14] Or, perhaps, he passed on our defector because, by the late sixties, Buckley considered blatant anti-communism passé; he now focused American conservatism on its new common enemy—namely, "liberalism."[15] Perhaps Buckley suspected that, with our defector, Steibel wanted to divert the show's attention back to the old foe and to spare liberalism a few blows, at least for a night. (Curiously, no such politics as "liberalism" still exists. What was once "liberalism" has since become an *illiberal* leftism on the one hand, and a growing body of defectors from illiberal leftism, on the other.)

Of course, another possible explanation for the decision not to have our former Soviet citizen on *Firing Line* must be considered. Perhaps the agency had gotten wind of the possibility, and thwarted it. Perhaps they wanted to protect our defector's value as a relatively secret U.S. intelligence asset.

Likewise, he remained unknown to the vast majority of U.S citizens, although his defection preceded that of Anatoliy Golitsyn (1961) and Yuri Nosenko (1964), as well as the expulsion of Solzhenitsyn (1974). And, his well-articulated anti-communism was derived from an intimate and in-depth knowledge of Marxist-Leninist theory—which he'd studied under the Bolsheviks for many years before the Revolution—but also a knowledge of Soviet, and, through extensive reading of news and other reports, Maoist "praxis." Furthermore, as the agency represented it, he was about to undergo an unprecedented world-historical techno-transfer *vis-à-vis* a technology that would not be released to the public for at least seventy-five years

---

14　In his autobiography in 1998, Buckley called Chambers "the most important American defector from Communism." Buckley, William F. *Nearer, My God: an Autobiography of Faith*. Harcourt Brace, 1998, p. 79. Later, on July 9, 2001, he eulogized Chambers at a special White House ceremony honoring Chambers on the fortieth anniversary of his death: Foreword to the Fiftieth Anniversary Edition, "Witness and Friend: Remembering Whittaker Chambers," by William F. Buckley Jr. Chambers, Whittaker. *Witness* (Cold War Classics). Regnery History. Kindle Edition. Chambers died on July 9, 1961.

15　Edwards, Lee. "William F. Buckley Jr.: Conservative Icon." *The Heritage Foundation*, www.heritage.org/political-process/report/william-f-buckley-jr-conservative-icon.

(2043). His mission somehow was made to seem more improbable than the moon landing scheduled to take place in July of the following year. Why wasn't he considered the world's most important defector from communism? The answer is that he was not only *truly* knowledgeable; he knew too much.

What about his former self, the "possible" former self, whom he was to (re)visit in the Gulag—by means of televisual transport into a digitized past? Why were the agents so careful, always making sure to refer to this former self as a "possible" former self? What possibilities did their phrasing imply? They seemed to suggest that by intervening in the past that they might possibly alter it, while also threatening to alter the future, or what stood in relation to the past as future. Might he inadvertently so change the past such that his current existence might become an impossibility? If so, what, if anything, might he, himself, become? And if changed, or even if not, what might happen to his "possible" former self? Could and would his former self resist him? Or might he find himself having to resist his former self?

He knew the answers to these questions, even if the agents didn't, or didn't let on. The questions were based on unfounded assumptions. Either the agents chose their words carefully due to possibilities that they did not understand, or they intentionally misrepresented such possibilities in order to inflate the importance of the mission and perhaps his own self-importance. He'd figured this out in a matter of minutes after their announcement on May 9th. The interactivity suggested was impossible given the technology of digital time-travel, even if it had been a thousand years ahead of its time. He'd followed the relevant technological and scientific developments closely for almost two decades and easily extrapolated from the reported state of affairs. The agents confounded virtual or digital time travel with travel along a spacetime curvature or through a wormhole shortcut. In the former, one visited a record of past time and could have no more effect on it than a ghost on the material world. One would be unable to alter the past world in the slightest, or even gain the recognition of those who lived in the time block visited. One would see but remain unseen, unable to leave even a trace of one's existence among the inhabitants visited.

However, although digital time travel could not affect the past *per se*, it could change history! How was this apparent contradiction possible? It's not a contradiction. History is not synonymous with the past. History is knowledge or understanding of the past, a representation of it. All of the major ruling bodies and persons have known and manipulated history for this very reason—it is the only available representation of the past, at least at present, and as such it may pass for the past.

1968 was a watermark year for computing, networking, and communications technologies, as well as for Western leftist politics. Hewlett-Packard introduced the first personal computer; Robert Noyce and Gordon Moore founded Intel, the most important manufacturer of computing processers; Douglas Engelbart demonstrated hypertext, the basis for web links that together now comprise the World Wide Web; the Advanced Research Projects Agency Network (ARPANET), funded by the Advanced Research Projects Agency (ARPA), later renamed to the Defense Advanced Research Projects Agency (DARPA), released a Wide Area Network (WAN) that would become the Internet.

To top off an already momentous year, Engelbart, William R. English, and others, under the aegis of the Stanford Research Institute, released The Mother of all Demos, developed by the Research Center for Augmenting Human Intellect. The project was sponsored by ARPA, the National Aeronautics and Space Agency, and the Rome Air Development Center (Airforce). On December 9, 1968, at the Fall Joint Computer Conference in San Francisco, Engelbart and team unveiled the system. The user interfaces for the computing processes were displayed by a high-powered TV projector onto a large external screen. Engelbart demonstrated a computer station with windows (representations of different running programs bounded by graphical user interfaces (GUIs)), hypertext, and videoconferencing, linked to an online system with other computers.

The computer station and networked system had been up and running seven months earlier, by the time Agents 1 and 2 paid our Soviet defector a visit in May. In fact, the system Englehart displayed as the Mother of all Demos represented a minimalist version of a much more capable system than the one exhibited for public consumption.

This brings us back to William Shockley. What he was up to at Shockley Semiconductor? After setting up the Laboratory, assembling a team of physicists and engineers intent on developing and mass-producing transistors, and after Beckman paid $25,000 for a license to produce the patented transistors developed at Bell Labs by Bardeen and Brattain, it was the company's, and most importantly Shockley's plan, based on his Semiconductor theory, that the company would produce silicon transistors and easily find a market for them.

Shockley soon appeared to go off the rails. For some unknown reason, Shockley changed his mind and instead directed the company to build a four-layer diode, a device he worked on at Bell Labs. His insistence on producing four-layer diodes rather than salable transistors appeared to be nothing short of self-sabotage.[16] No good reason for this change of plans was given and none was asked for. He had simply wanted to gamble on the so-called Shockley Diode. None were ready for production and none were ever produced for sale. Meanwhile, Gordon Moore and Robert Noyce had already left Fairchild and established Intel, soon becoming billionaires.[17] Shockley saw no such money, despite the fact that the whole relocation of transistors, and the development of integrated circuits and semiconductors were his brainchildren. Shockley Semiconductor was sold at least twice, after losing an estimated $750,000 to $1,000,00 per year. The last owner was International Telephone & Telegraph Co., "which announced it was moving the firm to Florida (demonstrating how much they understood the business),"[18]

---

16  Shurkin, Joel N. *Broken Genius*, p. 171.

17  Quinones, Eric R. GalvanizeOpenSource/Tableau-Workshop. *Mercury News*, 29 Sept. 1997, p. 6A.

18  Shurkin, Joel N. *Broken Genius*, p. 87.

where it soon disbanded.

So just what did Shockley do with his time as his company was ostensibly falling to pieces, losing money hand over fist? As a fierce competitor, Shockley didn't have the disposition to stand by idly as his former employees became billionaires while he sank into oblivion; techies wondered how he seemed to accept his abject failure business-wise as compared to the astronomical successes of his "fair children," as the formerly Shockley employees who fled to Fairchild and then spread elsewhere came to be called. It seemed as if Shockley intentionally tanked Shockley Semiconductor. But why?

Like our defector, Shockley also might be characterized as a transistor. That is, when a current was applied to him, he resisted, deflected, and diverted it into another direction. The intervention of some switching agency must have also been involved. Otherwise, Shockley would have defended himself much more vehemently for his apparent peccadilloes and indiscretions where business matters were concerned, or would not have made such mistakes in the first place. Also, like a transistor, he amplified the circuit that had been applied to him, making his efforts all the more significant in the area into which they were diverted. Similarly, he would amplify the circuit that that apparently had been expected to conduct itself through him straight-forwardly, to follow a trajectory expected. His military education may have equipped him for a call to service of enormous consequences, one that far outstripped his dream of commercial success, and could very well explain why he folded the business just after he'd gotten his big break.

We now know that William Shockley, during what would have been an otherwise inexplicable period of dormancy, developed the digital time travel machine that would be become the vehicle for our defector to revisit the Gulag and his former self.[19] Further, we know that it included all of the features demonstrated in the Mother of All Demos, plus many more.

---

19 Shockley's eugenicist and racist period is well known. He was not chosen to be the architect of the Digital Time Machine because of these obsessions but as part of the agency's attempts redirect him from such obsessions.

Not only was it fully transistorized, it could run multiple programs simultaneously from RAM and the running programs were represented by GUIs. It was capable of video-conferencing, and of re-running analog recordings and converting them into digital audio-visual, and in fact, 3-D format. It was networked with other computers across a wide-area network, was hypertext-capable, could share and run programs residing on the CPU of networked partners, and was attached to and drew instantly from a vast remote digital storage space. Its monitor was a giant TV projector that produced 3-D imaging using distributed graphics and three screens. Last but not least, it was part of Wide Area Remote Surveillance system far more sophisticated than believed at the time. It consisted of far more cameras and other inputs than known and was able to process analogue film and convert it into the digital realm that our defector would encounter.

The means by which the digital data were obtained included films from within the Gulag taken by the Soviets and obtained by U.S. espionage, footage from U.S. planes flying over the Soviet Union, footage from the Wide Area Remote Surveillance system, and one or two unknown sources.

The agency wanted no significant lapse in time between their announcement of the program and its occurrence. Likewise, on May 10th, 1968, at 11 AM, the agents arrived at our defector's door and used the brass knocker. No delay followed their knock and the appearance of our transistor this time.

They drove to Shockley Semiconductor, less than ten minutes away. When they arrived, William Shockley was standing on the unkempt grass lawn in front of the building. Barely making acquaintance with our transistor, he ushered him and the agents into the building. They entered a room. It was large and dark. After a few minutes, our resistor could see the white screens that lined the back and two side walls. Then the computer station became visible and he was directed by Shockley to take the seat.

Soon, the digital past began to roll on three-sides in 3-D. But the images were black-and-white, very grainy, and ghost-like. He could barely make himself out but he finally found himself. He was emaciated, dirty, and looked as if his face was about to fall off at any second. Yet, he was wielding an axe, cutting at the trunk of a tree, stopping every few strokes to take a break, to wipe his brow, and begin again. The tree seemed endless, as if cutting through it would take an eternity.

The scene changed to inside the Gulag center, to the sleeping quarters. There he was, lying in a bunkbed, scribbling rapidly on a notebook, at seemingly super-human speed. He seemed frantic—not only to write but to conceal the fact that he was writing. Soon he ditched the notebook and pen under his pillow. A guard must have been approaching.

There was more and more footage like this. The exhibition went on for forty minutes. But after getting the picture, our resistor wondered what purpose this display could possibly serve, other than to sadden him beyond words. The technology was poor. His life had been worse than poor. Rather than making him feel a sense of relief and gratitude that such a life was behind him, the exhibition served to degrade his current life, to degrade all life. If life could be so horrible, what could one possibly celebrate? And although this was likely not the intention, the semi-immersion into his past life, even if only through a very incomplete digital archive, felt like sadism. He felt as if freedom and unfreedom were equally overrated—but only because unfreedom existed. Freedom, he thought, should be such a norm that such aberrations and interruptions of it should be impossible in the first place. And thus, he would soldier on.

# New Knowledge, or Does "the Real" Exist?

I BEGIN THIS CONCLUSION with a discussion of the digital simulacrum—or the way that the digital realm has produced a simulated reality that makes distinguishing between simulated realities and actual realities almost impossible for the denizens of the Internet, the Internet of "everyware."[1] I then enter a brief discussion on the metaphysics of truth, and end with a final jab at Google, for good measure, and for good reasons.

Social reality has always been a result of human social activity, and thus, in this sense, all social reality has always been a social production. This is not the same as saying that reality is a "social construction," which places reality formation primarily if not entirely in the collective (or individual) minds of the beholder, rather than as an objective correlative of perception, cognition, and reflection. But the difference in the digital sphere and non-simulacra is that social realities can be produced that appear to involve real social actors and their activities, yet which are the results of digitization and its manipulation, creating simulations which compete with and displace legitimately produced social realities. At this stage, the architects of Big Digital

---

1  Greenfield, Adam. *Everyware: the Dawning Age of Ubiquitous Computing.* New Riders, 2006.

161

produce faux realities, while the major principals simultaneously smear anyone who counters their narratives or disputes their simulacra as conspiracy theorists. To concretize this discussion, I will focus on one particular player in the realm of Big Digital: "New Knowledge."

Within the Big Digital Simulacrum, information, knowledge and "reality" are shaped through disinformation agents and ideological filters. Paradoxically and almost mind-bendingly beyond belief, the primary disinformation agents are the very same principals who claim to be delivering unfiltered reality, who claim to be the major information and anti-disinformation agents of the digital sphere, and who are generally regarded as such. A parallel can be drawn between the "the information integrity" organization known as New Knowledge,[2] and the Big Digital super power, Google. New Knowledge is to disinformation what Google is to information.

"Russiagate" must be understood as probably the first major combined effort by the political establishment, the mass media, and Big Digital to produce and promote a fictional narrative, a simulated reality, and to deem anyone who refused, denied, or countered said narrative a Russian bot, or worse. The narrative dominated the media headlines and social media algorithms for nearly three years. Yet a seldom discussed but nonetheless intriguing character in the simulacrum or fictional-narrative-floated-as-reality known as Russiagate is an organization that one might call a double agent where digital narrative constructions are concerned—the mysterious "New Knowledge." After playing superhero for the U.S. Senate Intelligence Committee, a role that might have qualified the digital organization for the leading role in "The Spy Who Loved Me," where "Me" was "social media integrity" and the U.S. electorate, New Knowledge soon engaged in a "political experiment" that revealed the organization to be double agents, at least in terms of reality itself, if not in terms of the national interest.

New Knowledge is an organization made up of former intel-

---

2 "Something Is Wrong on the Internet." *New Knowledge*, www.newknowledge.com/.

ligence officers, state officials, and former Big Digital engineers. It presents itself as a kind of new age social media police force. Its stated mission is to "detect, monitor, and mitigate social media manipulation." First, it warns the reader, who happens upon its website, in disturbingly smeared text:

**Homepage of New Knowledge**

"Uh-oh," the hapless website visitor thinks. "God, now what?" The implication is that every other website that one has encountered has been "wrong," and you, dear reader, have been the unwitting dupe of whatever it is. Scrolling down through considerable black space, one finally comes to a brief and startling statement of the problem:

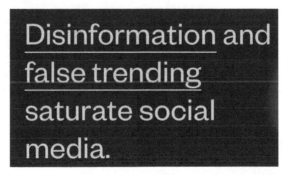

**The problem with social media per New Knowledge**

Of course, the stage is set for the solution, which is, of

course, New Knowledge itself. One has little choice but to click on the menu links to learn more, because this league of digital media geniuses knows just how to steer you to a conclusion: there is nothing else on the home page. So, one might click on the "About Us" link to get clued-in on the Big Secret:

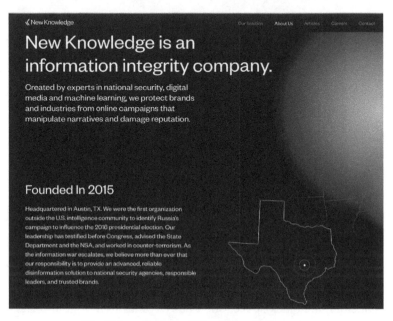

The "About" page of NewKnowledge.com

Presenting itself as the "first organization outside of the U.S. intelligence community to identify Russia's campaign to influence the 2016 presidential election," New Knowledge authored the second of two reports to the Senate Intelligence Committee, providing extensive evidence of Russian social media manipulation to support Trump's candidacy.[3] In particular, the report headed by New Knowledge found that "YouTube offered some new statistics, including that the Russians posted more

_____

3  DiResta, Renee, et al. *New Knowledge: The Tactics & Tropes of the Internet Research Agency.* New Knowledge, 18 Dec. 2018, disinformationreport. blob.core.windows.net/disinformation-report/NewKnowledge-Disinformation-Report-Whitepaper.pdf.

than 1,000 YouTube videos for their disinformation campaign and that Instagram generated more than twice the 'engagement' among users than either Facebook or Twitter."[4]

Despite its self-presentation as arbiters and exposers of fake news and social media manipulation, in 2018, the *New York Times*[5] and the *Washington Post*[6] both published, rather uncharacteristically for Democratic Party organs, articles that uncovered a social media "experiment" undertaken by New Knowledge. The articles detailed how New Knowledge itself created fake Russian bots as supporters of former Chief Justice Roy S. Moore of Alabama in the 2017 election for the U.S. Senate—in order to give the impression that the Kremlin was behind the candidacy of Roy Moore!

New Knowledge claimed that this was simply an experiment in understanding how Russian disinformation agents operate. But not only had New Knowledge created the supposed "Russian bots" that plied and pled for Moore supporters, it actually fed "collusion" reports about "Russian bots" to the U.S. Senate, while simultaneously disseminating "news" of this "collusion" throughout the mainstream media, mainly via Big Digital algorithms.

New Knowledge is a Big Digital agency directly involved in disinformation, even while continuing to pose as an anti-disinformation agent. The New Knowledge website is still "up and running." Despite the significant dissimulation that New Knowledge has already perpetrated, the organization retains

---

4 Timberg, Craig, and Tony Romm. "New Report on Russian Disinformation, Prepared for the Senate, Shows the Operation's Scale and Sweep." *The Washington Post*, WP Company, 17 Dec. 2018, www.washingtonpost.com/technology/2018/12/16/new-report-russian-disinformation-prepared-senate-shows-operations-scale-sweep/?noredirect=on.

5 Shane, Scott, and Alan Blinder. "Secret Experiment in Alabama Senate Race Imitated Russian Tactics." *The New York Times*, The New York Times, 20 Dec. 2018, www.nytimes.com/2018/12/19/us/alabama-senate-roy-jones-russia.html.

6 Craig Timberg, et al. "Secret Bid to Affect Vote in Ala. Rattles Democrats." *The Washington Post*, 2019 July 1AD. EBSCOhost, search.ebscohost.com/login.aspx?direct=true&db=bwh&AN=wapo.58803f26-0400-11e9-8186-4ec26a485713&site=eds-live.

Twitter[7] and Facebook[8] accounts. Although its CEO, Jonathon Morgan, had his Facebook account suspended,[9] Morgan retains a verified Twitter account.[10]

Morgan admittedly has already tampered with a U.S. senatorial election by simulating a Russian bot scenario, while incredibly spreading disinformation about such a simulated reality as "news." He made up a crisis and then spread "information" about the crisis as "news."

Compare Big Digital's treatment of Morgan with that of one Jacob Wohl, a Trump supporter, who announced his intentions to create "'enormous left-wing properties,' including Facebook and Twitter accounts, before the 2020 presidential election in order 'to steer the left-wing votes in the primaries to what we feel are weaker candidates compared with Trump.'"[11] Note: the 2020 election has not happened, and Wohl had not yet spread disinformation, let alone created a faux reality that he then promoted as "news." Wohl's crime was to (stupidly) telegraph his intentions, while Morgan had already done the deeds. While Wohl's Twitter account was terminated, Morgan's account is still active *and verified,* and New Knowledge's Twitter account is still operative. The organization continues to bill itself on Twitter as "an information integrity company. We protect brands and industries from manipulative online campaigns." This is like a group of bank robbers advertising their organization as "a

---

7  Knowledge, New. "New Knowledge (@NewKnowledgeAI)." *Twitter*, Twitter, 17 Dec. 2018, twitter.com/NewKnowledgeAI,

8  "New Knowledge." Facebook, www.facebook.com/newknowledgeai/.

9  Hoffower, Hillary. "Facebook suspended five accounts for spreading misleading information during an Alabama election, including a lead social media researcher who helped the government discover fake news." *Business Insider*, Dec. 22, 2018. https://www.businessinsider.com/facebook-suspends-account-of-jonathon-morgan-new-knowledge-ceo-2018-12,

10  Account, Jonathon Morgan, Verified. "Jonathon Morgan (@Jonathonmorgan)." *Twitter*, Twitter, 2 Aug. 2019, twitter.com/jonathonmorgan.

11  Garcia-Roberts, Gus. "Twitter Bans Trump-Supporting Hoaxster after USA TODAY Exposé." *USA Today*, Gannett Satellite Information Network, 27 Feb. 2019, www.usatoday.com/story/news/investigations/2019/02/26/jacob-wohl-spread-lies-mueller-rbg-twitter-just-banned-him/2995037002/.

banking security company."

Furthermore, New Knowledge provides even more evidence of the blatant political character of Big Digital. While the New Knowledge "experiment" was funded by Big Digital billionaire, LinkedIn co-founder, early Facebook investor, and donor of multi-millions to Democratic causes and candidacies, Reid Hoffman,[12] it has recently garnered three million dollars in funding from the city of Austin, TX, "to expand its technology aimed at stopping fake news and protecting clients from disinformation campaigns."[13] Wow.

What might we conclude, not only about the company that literally goes by the name "New Knowledge," but also about much of what passes as "new knowledge" in the digital realm? In that new knowledge is reporting about a simulacrum created by the reporters themselves, new knowledge represents not only a new nescience, or lack of knowledge, but new knowledge is actually worse than ignorance. Within Big Digital, new knowledge produces substitutes for reality and reports on such substitutes as if they were real. New knowledge amounts to simulated realities with simulated information to support them. Within Big Digital, or the Google Archipelago, new knowledge is a fraud on public credulity, a lying sham, a pretended reality, and a production of sinister megalomaniacs.

New knowledge must be countered, not only with real knowledge, but with a metaphysics of truth. By this I mean not merely a rejuvenated quest for the truth, but more fundamentally the re-establishment of a framework or frameworks for knowing and approaching the truth. Such projects have generally been confined to philosophers but must now extend to the entire populace. Such reestablishment of a metaphysics of truth

---

12  Feiner, Lauren. "Reid Hoffman Apologizes for Funding a Group That Allegedly Spread Misinformation in Alabama Senate Race." CNBC, CNBC, 26 Dec. 2018, https://www.cnbc.com/2018/12/26/reid-hoffman-apologizes-for-his-role-in-funding-misinformation.html.

13  Hawkins, Lori. "Austin Cybersecurity Firm New Knowledge Lands $3M for Expansion." *Statesman*, Austin American-Statesman, 31 July 2019, www.statesman.com/news/20190730/austin-cybersecurity-firm-new-knowledge-lands-3m-for-expansion.

will be particularly difficult in a world of virtual realities, digital simulacra, smart cities, and a stupefied population, mostly through no fault of its own.

But whatever the difficulties, the project must be undertaken. It begins with resisting the simulacra and fabrications of the Google Archipelago, just as our defector resisted communism and the Gulag. Resistance will include rejecting the narratives of the Google Archipelago, with its smart cities and simulated realities; narratives that tell us that we are a mere series of digits.

The nineteenth century reduced the world to mere matter. The twentieth century reduced human beings to material machines constructed of flesh and bone. When materialism reigns, and there is nothing but matter, then literally nothing matters, including human life. Now, the twenty-first century would reduce us to zeros and ones—or, that is, to zeros, period. We must counter this false narrative with truth that restores us to our true natures as beings of value far beyond what the materialists and now the digital reductionists would have us believe.

Otherwise, the least of our problems will be something like Epcot Center passing for Europe. For what shall it profit a man, if he should gain the whole world, a simulated world at that, while he loses his soul? The worst case scenario, at least in this realm, might be fake apps and sock-puppets passing for "Russian bots," with nuclear reactionaries responding in kind— the consequence of shysters producing fake realities and then hysterically promoting fake news about such fake realities, all for personal and political "gain." The powers and principalities might thereby coalesce to prove that the world is nothing— nothing but zeros and ones, and the inhabitants thereof, zeros.

And not only would such prestidigitation jeopardize the perpetrators' souls but also the lives of the world's inhabitants, and thus condemn the perpetrators to whatever awaits mass deceivers and mass murderers on an unparalleled scale. Far be it for me to say just what that might be, but I would imagine that it won't be pleasant.

∽

So that I don't end on a such dour note, let's have some fun with Google. Following are two Google searches and the top suggestions they yield. You may have heard of this search exercise, but consider it now in the context of the simulacra of the Google Archipelago. There, now I've gone and taken the fun out of it. But here is fun with Google, as far as it goes:

# Google

Q  men can

Q  men can **have babies**

Q  men can

Q  men can**cer**

Q  men can **get pregnant**

Q  men can **have babies now**

Q  men can**vas shoes**

Q  men can**dles**

Q  men can **cook**

Q  men can**'t have babies**

Q  men can**'t multitask**

Google Search     I'm Feeling Lucky

*Report inappropriate predictions*

# Google

| | |
|---|---|
| Q | women can |

| | |
|---|---|
| Q | women can |
| Q | women can **fly** |
| Q | women can**cer** |
| Q | women can **vote** |
| Q | women can **do it** |
| Q | women can**vas shoes** |
| Q | women can**dle company** |
| Q | women can **do anything** |
| Q | women can**didates** |
| Q | women can**didates for president** |

Google Search     I'm Feeling Lucky

*Report inappropriate predictions*

# Appendix A

## Additional Articles Not Sourced in Main Text

Alexander, Julia. "YouTube Terminates Channel Dedicated to Circumventing Alex Jones Ban." *The Verge*, The Verge, 19 Mar. 2019, https://www.theverge.com/2019/3/19/18272690/ alex-jones-youtube-ban-info-wars-resistance-news.

YouTube has terminated an account that was seemingly operating as a secondary channel for Alex Jones and Infowars after its first one was banned last August. A statement from YouTube confirmed that the channel, "Resistance News, was banned for aiding in Jones' ban evasion...YouTube will remove channels that are dedicated to live-streaming Infowars content or uploading videos of full Infowars live streams without additional context or commentary."

Ali, Idrees, and Patricia Zengerle. "Google's Work in China Benefiting China's Military: U.S. General." *Reuters*, Thomson Reuters, 14 Mar. 2019, https://www.reuters.com/article/us-usa-china-google/googles-work-in-china-benefiting-chinas-military-u-s-general-idUSKCN1QV296.

The United States' top general said on Thursday that the

Chinese military was benefiting from the work Alphabet Inc's Google was doing in China, where the technology giant has long sought to have a bigger presence. "The work that Google is doing in China is indirectly benefiting the Chinese military," Marine General Joseph Dunford, chairman of the Joint Chiefs of Staff, said during a Senate Armed Services Committee hearing.

Birnbaum, Emily. "Tulsi Gabbard Sues Google over Censorship Claims." *The Hill*, The Hill, 25 July 2019, https://thehill. com/policy/technology/454746-tulsi-gabbard-sues-google-over-censorship-claims.

Rep. Tulsi Gabbard (D-Hawaii), a 2020 presidential contender, is suing Google over claims that the tech behemoth violated her right to "free speech." In a federal complaint filed Thursday in the U.S. District Court for the Central District of California, Gabbard alleged Google censored her presidential campaign when it suspended their advertising account for several hours last month.

Bokhari, Allum. "Exclusive: Facebook's Process to Label You a 'Hate Agent' Revealed." *Breitbart*, 13 June 2019, https:// www.breitbart.com/tech/2019/06/13/exclusive-facebooks-process-to-label-you-a-hate-agent-revealed/.

Facebook monitors the offline behavior of its users to determine if they should be categorized as a "Hate Agent," according to a document provided exclusively to Breitbart News by a source within the social media giant. The document, titled "Hate Agent Policy Review," outlines a series of "signals" that Facebook uses to determine if someone ought to be categorized as a "hate agent" and banned from the platform. Those signals include a wide range of on- and off-platform behavior. If you praise the wrong individual, interview them, or appear at events alongside them, Facebook may categorize you as a "hate agent."

Copeland, Rob. "Fired by Google, a Republican Engineer Hits Back: 'There's Been a Lot of Bullying.'" *The Wall Street Journal*, Dow Jones & Company, 1 Aug. 2019, https://www.wsj. com/articles/fired-by-google-a-republican-engineer-hits-back-theres-been-a-lot-of-bullying-11564651801.

Search giant's culture wars flame anew; a senior executive contacts law enforcement over leaks. Kevin Cernekee was still a "Noogler"—Google's term for a new employee—when his conservative take on political and social issues raised hackles within the search giant. After several posts on the company's freewheeling internal message boards in early 2015 rankled some colleagues, he was given an official warning from human resources about conduct deemed disrespectful and insubordinate. Around that time, a senior manager wrote on the boards that he added Mr. Cernekee to a "written blacklist" of employees...

D'Abrosca, Peter. "EXCLUSIVE: Congressional Candidate Banned From Instagram, Calls for FEC Investigation." *The Rundown News*, 31 July 2019, https://therundown-news.com/2019/07/exclusive-congressional-candi-date-banned-from-instagram-calls-for-fec-investigation/.

Facebook-owned Instagram has banned a Republican candidate for U.S. Congress from using its platform. "Your account has been disabled for violating our terms," Instagram said in an automated message to Tom Norton's campaign account. Norton is a Republican seeking to primary recently-turned Independent Rep. Justin Amash of Michigan's 3rd Congressional District, who quit the Republican party in a hissy fit over President Donald J. Trump.

Dunleavy, Jerry. "Google Shut down Chinese Censorship Project but Won't Rule out Working with China." *Washington Examiner*, 16 July 2019, https://www.washingtonexaminer. com/news/google-shut-down-chinese-censorship-project-but-wont-rule-out-working-with-china.

A top Google executive revealed today that the global tech firm had shut down its effort to build a search engine that would comply with the repressive censorship requirements of the Communist Chinese regime. But Karan Bhatia would not commit to Google never attempting another such censorship project in China in the future in a tense exchange with Sen. Josh Hawley. The vice president and global head of government affairs and public policy at Google was grilled Tuesday in front of the Senate Judiciary Subcommittee on the Constitution by the Missouri Republican during a hearing focused on Google and allegations of suppressing conservative viewpoints.

Ellis, John. "Facebook Bans St. Augustine Quote as 'Hate Speech.'" *PJ Media*, 16 July 2019, https://pjmedia.com/faith/facebook-bans-st-augustine-quote-as-hate-speech/.

The Director of Community Engagements for Massachusetts Citizens for Life claims that Facebook has labeled a quote by St. Augustine as hate speech. In a blog post, Domenico Bettinelli wrote, "Facebook has repeatedly banned a quote from St. Augustine every time I've posted it. And it's not some fire and brimstone 'Sinners are going to hell!' quote, but in fact, quite the opposite."

Eustachewich, Lia. "Google Engineer Claims He Was Bullied, Fired for Being a Conservative." *New York Post*, New York Post, 1 Aug. 2019, https://nypost.com/2019/08/01/google-engineer-claims-he-was-bullied-fired-for-being-a-conservative/.

An ousted conservative Google engineer claims he was the victim of the tech giant's systematic "bullying" of its more right-leaning employees, according to a new report. Trump supporter Kevin Cernekee was fired from the liberal Silicon Valley company in June 2018, which he alleges was over his outspoken criticism on internal message boards of others with opposing views, the *Wall Street Journal* reported on Thursday. "Historically, there's been a lot of bullying at Google," Cernekee said. "There's a big political angle, and they treat the two sides very differently."

Hall, Alexander. "Instagram Mysteriously Purges Popular Meme Pages." *NewsBusters*, 2 Aug. 2019, https://www.newsbusters.org/blogs/techwatch/alexander-hall/2019/08/02/instagram-mysteriously-purges-popular-meme-pages.

Instagram has gone to war with meme pages. The reason why is unclear. "Instagram seems to have purged most of the top meme accounts on the platform," according to *Insider*. Reports indicate that pages with hundreds of thousands to millions of followers were suddenly purged on July 25 and 26. YouTuber and free speech advocate Tim Pool theorized in his video "The Great Meme PURGE Is Upon Us, Instagram BANNED 30+ Accounts" that this may be a calculated move ahead of the 2020 election.

Hamill, Jasper. "Twitter Admits Filtering 600,000 Accounts Including Some Owned by Politicians." Metro, Metro.co.uk, 6 Sept. 2018, https://metro.co.uk/2018/09/06/twitter-admits-shadowbanning-and-unfairly-filtering-600000-accounts-7920206/.

Twitter's systems unfairly filtered 600,000 accounts including some belonging to members of Congress, chief executive Jack Dorsey has admitted. He made the confession during an opening statement on Wednesday to the US House Energy and Commerce Committee, which is looking into the social network's algorithms and content monitoring. The Twitter boss said the company's algorithms were to blame for hiding some members from its auto-complete search and latest results but had since fixed the issue.

Kendall, Brent. "Justice Department to Open Broad, New Antitrust Review of Big Tech Companies." *The Wall Street Journal*, Dow Jones & Company, 23 July 2019, https://www.wsj. com/articles/justice-department-to-open-broad-new-antitrust-review-of-big-tech-companies-11563914235.

The Justice Department is opening a broad antitrust review into whether dominant technology firms are unlawfully stifling competition, adding a new Washington threat for companies such as Facebook Inc., Google, Amazon.com Inc. and Apple Inc. The review is geared toward examining the practices of online platforms that dominate internet search, social media and retail services, the department said, confirming the review shortly after The Wall Street Journal reported it.

MacDonald, Cheyenne. "Instagram Will Warn You If You Are about to Be Rude! Firm Rolls out New Anti-Bullying Measures." *Daily Mail Online*, Associated Newspapers, 8 July 2019, https://www.dailymail.co.uk/sciencetech/article-7226019/Instagram-rolls-anti-bullying-feature-lets-users-block-comments-specific-people.html.

[Instagram] revealed on Monday that it has begun rolling out an AI-powered tool that will notify users if the comment they're about to post may be 'considered offensive.' This will give that person a chance to review their comment and potentially reconsider. Instagram has also added a new feature called Restrict that will give users greater control over the comments that appear on their posts, allowing you to hide comments from specific people without them finding out.

Madden, Nate. "The Department of Justice Will Investigate Silicon Valley Companies for Violations of Monopoly Law." *Conservative Review*, 24 July 2019, https://www.conservativereview.com/news/department-justice-will-investigate-silicon-valley-companies-violations-monopoly-law/.

The Department of Justice division dedicated to investigating violations of antitrust and monopoly laws will take a look at how big tech platforms have been doing business, according to a press release sent out late Tuesday afternoon. The DOJ release explained that the probe "will consider the widespread concerns that consumers, businesses, and entrepreneurs have expressed about search, social media, and some retail services online." ...The press release mentions no companies specifically as investigation subjects, suggesting a wide-ranging investigation.

Mercola, Joseph, MD. "Google Traffic to Mercola.com Plummets by 99% Part 1." *Mercola.com*, 24 June 2019, https://articles.mercola.com/sites/articles/archive/2019/06/24/google-latest-algorithm-update-buries-mercola.aspx.

This year, we've seen an unprecedented push to implement censorship across all online platforms, making obtaining and sharing crucial information about health in general, and vaccines in particular, increasingly difficult. Google's June 2019 update, which took effect June 3, has effectively removed Mercola.com from Google search results. If undesirable pages don't vanish automatically in the new algorithm, Google's quality raters will manually manipulate crowdsourced relevance to bury the page or pages.

Ng, David. "Gillette Loses $8 Billion as Sales Drop Following Woke Commercials." *Breitbart*, 2 Aug. 2019, https://www.breitbart.com/economy/2019/08/02/gillette-loses-8-billion-as-sales-drop-following-woke-commercials/.

Gillette experienced a whopping $8 billion write-down during its most recent quarter, the latest setback for the maker of razors and other personal grooming supplies... Gillette helped to drag P&G into the red for the fiscal fourth quarter, with a net loss of $5.24 billion for the consumer goods giant, compared to net income of $1.89 billion a year ago. Gillette generated heated social media pushback earlier this year after it debuted a series of commercials that criticized masculinity and featured a transgender adolescent learning to shave.

Nieva, Richard. "Peter Thiel Says Google's AI Work in China Is 'Bad for America.'" CNET, CNET, 2 Aug. 2019, https://www.cnet.com/news/peter-thiel-says-googles-ai-work-in-china-is-bad-for-america/.

Last month the investor said Google has a "seemingly treasonous" relationship with China. Now, in a New York Times op-ed, he's underlining his point. --Peter Thiel is doubling down on his criticism of Google. The Silicon Valley investor wrote in a New York Times op-ed Thursday that the search giant is hurting the US by sharing its artificial intelligence technology with China...He wrote that AI is "valuable to any army -- to gain an intelligence advantage, for example, or to penetrate defenses in the relatively new theater of cyberwarfare, where we are already living amid the equivalent of a multinational shooting war."

O'Sullivan, Donie. "Twitter Suspends Account Hours after Trump Retweeted It." *CNN*, Cable News Network, 30 July 2019, https://www.cnn.com/2019/07/30/politics/trump-retweet-twitter-account-deleted/index.html.

In a move that will likely embolden President Donald Trump's claims that social media companies are biased against him and his supporters, Twitter suspended an account Tuesday evening that the President had retweeted just hours earlier. Trump retweeted a post from an account operating under the name "Lynn Thomas" that accused Democrats of being "the true enemies of America." ...Just a few hours later, Twitter had suspended the account, confirming to CNN it had broken the platform's rules. The company did not say what rules the account had broken.

Price, Lori. "All CLGers Please Read, Regarding Google's Censorship of This Newsletter." *CLG News*, CLG News, 24 Jan. 2019, https://www.legitgov.org/All-CLGers-please-read-regarding-Googles-censorship-newsletter.

Here is a 'self-censored' resend of today's (24 January 2019) *CLG Newsletter*, as...Google relegated the original edition to the spam bin. It is interesting to note that I checked CLG's mail server IP via MxToolbox, and there is currently NO blacklisting of that IP. Ergo, it is GOOGLE, on its OWN, deciding that YOU should not receive this newsletter. Note: I had to remove several stories in this 'revised' edition, in order to try to circumvent Google's content sentinels.

Re, Gregg, and Catherine Herridge. "Nunes Sues Twitter, Some Users, Seeks over $250M Alleging Anti-Conservative 'Shadow Bans,' Smears." *Fox News*, FOX News Network, 19 Mar. 2019, https://www.foxnews.com/politics/nunes-files-bombshell-defamation-suit-against-twitter-seeks-250m-for-anti-conservative-shadow-bans-smears

California GOP Rep. Devin Nunes filed a major lawsuit seeking $250 million in compensatory damages and $350,000 in punitive damages against Twitter and a handful of its users on Monday, accusing the social media site of "shadow-banning conservatives" to secretly hide their posts, systematically censoring opposing viewpoints, and totally "ignoring" lawful complaints of repeated abusive behavior. In a complaint filed in Virginia state court on Monday, obtained by Fox News, Nunes claimed Twitter wanted to derail his work on the House Intelligence Committee, which he chaired until 2019, as he looked into alleged and apparent surveillance abuses by the government. Nunes said Twitter was guilty of "knowingly hosting and monetizing content that is clearly abusive, hateful and defamatory—providing both a voice and financial incentive to the defamers—thereby facilitating defamation on its platform."

Report, Staff. "BREAKING: Apple News Bans LifeSite without Warning: Says It 'Shows Intolerance.'" *LifeSiteNews*, LifeSite, 31 July 2019, https://www.lifesitenews.com/news/breaking-apple-news-bans-lifesite-without-warning-shows-intolerance.

A little over one week ago, Apple approved LifeSiteNews' application to publish our news on their Apple News platform. Today, without warning, Apple News abruptly reversed course, telling LifeSite that they had deleted our channel and all of our content from their platform. Apple claimed that LifeSite's channel "didn't comply with our Apple News guidelines." Specifically, they stated that LifeSite's "[c]hannel content shows intolerance towards a specific group."

Report, Staff. "Facebook Insider Leaks Docs; Explains 'Deboosting,' 'Troll Report,' & Political Targeting in Video Interview." *Project Veritas*, Project Veritas, 27 Feb. 2019, https://www.projectveritas.com/2019/02/27/facebook-insider-leaks-docs/.

Project Veritas has obtained and published documents and presentation materials from a former Facebook insider. This information describes how Facebook engineers plan and go about policing political speech. Screenshots from a Facebook workstation show the specific technical actions taken against political figures, as well as "[e]xisting strategies" taken to combat political speech.

Report, Staff. "Twitter Suspends Russian Embassy in Syria after It Criticized White Helmets." *RT International*, RT, 30 July 2019, https://www.rt.com/news/465424-russian-embassy-syria-twitter/.

Without explanation, Twitter has suspended the official account of the Russian embassy in Syria after it posted a video critical of the controversial 'White Helmets' group, citing statements by the Russian military. "Twitter suspends accounts that violate Twitter rules," said the default notice on the grayed-out page of @RusEmbSyria on Tuesday...[T] he Russian embassy in South Africa has chimed in, calling Twitter "thought police" for banning their colleagues. The account was banned after posting factual criticism of the 'White Helmets' quoting the Russian military, the embassy said.

Rider, David. "Sidewalk Labs' Project in Toronto Could Be Dead by October If Disagreements Persist." *The Star.com*, 2 Aug. 2019, https://www.thestar.com/news/gta/2019/08/02/ sidewalk-labs-project-in-toronto-could-be-dead-by-october-if-disagreements-persist.html.

Sidewalk Labs' role in remaking Toronto's east waterfront could end Oct. 31 if the Google sister company and Waterfront Toronto cannot resolve fundamental disagreements over plans for the globally watched project. The waterfront development agency representing the city, province and federal government and Sidewalk Labs have agreed on the Halloween deadline to address stumbling blocks on turning a 12-acre site dubbed Quayside, and possibly another 178 acres of public land to the east, into a living laboratory for the sustainable neighbourhood of the future.

Shaw, C. Mitchell. "Facebook Denies Shadow Banning, Receives Patent for Shadow Banning." *The New American*, 1 Aug. 2019, https://www.thenewamerican.com/tech/computers/item/32995-facebook-denies-shadow-banning-receives-patent-for-shadow-banning.

Facebook has continually denied that it participates in the practice of shadow banning—a method of blocking a users' posts or comments from everyone except the user who made the post or comment. But a newly granted patent shows that Facebook not only does practice shadow banning, but wants to protect—by patent—the method it uses for doing so. Despite the fact that Facebook executives denied the practice in congressional testimony in April, the company was awarded a patent by the U.S. Patent and Trademark Office (USPTO) earlier this month for an automated system that would "receive a list of proscribed content and block comments containing the proscribed content by reducing the distribution of those comments to other viewing users" while continuing to "display the blocked content to the commenting user such that the commenting user is not made aware that his or her comment was blocked." A better definition of shadow banning would be hard to write.

Shepardson, David, et al. "Trump Calls for Inquiry into Google's Work with China." *Reuters*, Thomson Reuters, 16 July 2019, https://www.reuters.com/article/us-google-trump/trump-calls-for-inquiry-into-googles-work-with-china-idUSKCN1UB1DE.

U.S. President Donald Trump said on Tuesday his administration would investigate whether Alphabet Inc's Google supports the Chinese government, following accusations that a company official refuted hours later at a Senate hearing. The president repeated accusations made previously by Peter Thiel, a co-founder of PayPal and venture capitalist, that Google may be infiltrated by Chinese intelligence agents...Trump later told reporters he would have various agencies, including potentially the Justice Department, "see if there's any truth to" Thiel's accusations.

Smith, Mikey. "Twitter Bans Tommy Robinson and Ukip Candidate Carl Benjamin's Campaign Accounts." *The Mirror*, 26 Apr. 2019, https://www.mirror.co.uk/news/politics/twitter-bans-tommy-robinson-ukip-14729717.

Both had already had their personal accounts banned from

the platform—but now their campaign accounts are also suspended. Twitter has banned the Euro election campaign accounts of Ukip candidate Carl Benjamin and far-right extremist Tommy Robinson.

Thiel, Peter. "Good for Google, Bad for America." *The New York Times*, The New York Times, 1 Aug. 2019, https://www.nytimes.com/2019/08/01/opinion/peter-thiel-google.html.

At its core, artificial intelligence is a military technology. Why is the company sharing it with a rival?—A "Manhattan Project" for artificial intelligence is how Dennis Hassabis, the founder of DeepMind, described his company in 2010, when I was one of its first investors. I took it as figurative grandiosity...Now almost a decade later, DeepMind is the crown jewel of Google's A.I. effort...A.I. is a military technology...A.I.'s military power is the simple reason that the recent behavior of America's leading software company, Google—starting an A.I. lab in China while ending an A.I. contract with the Pentagon—is shocking.

Tillison, Tom. "Expert, Hillary Supporter Warns Congress Google Manipulated Millions of Votes for Dems in 2016, Will 'Go All out' in 2020." *BizPac Review*, BizPac Review, 29 July 2019, https://www.bizpacreview.com/2019/07/29/expert-hillary-supporter-warns-congress-google-manipulated-millions-of-votes-for-dems-in-2016-will-go-all-out-in-2020-779664.

Dr. Robert Epstein, a liberal professor and self-avowed "strong public supporter of Hillary Clinton," testified recently before the Senate Judiciary Subcommittee on the Constitution and gave a startling assessment of voter manipulation in the 2016 election. Manipulation not by Russia, but by Google and, to a lessor [sic] extent, Facebook. "You testified before this committee that Google's manipulation of votes gave at least 2.6 million additional votes to Hillary

Clinton in the year 2016, is that correct?" asked Sen. Ted Cruz (R-TX) at the hearing. "That's correct," replied Epstein, the former editor-in-chief of *Psychology Today*.

TiredOfLyingForGoogle. "I Helped Google Screw over James Damore." *Reddit*, Feb. 2019, https://www.reddit.com/r/JamesDamore/comments/adpj0h/i_helped_google_screw_over_james_damore/.

I was involved in the internal decisions involving James Damore's memo, and it's terrible what we did to him. First of all, we knew about the memo a month before it went viral. HR sent it up the reporting chain when he gave it as internal feedback, but we did nothing. There wasn't anything we could do, except admit to wrongdoing and lying to our employees. We just hoped that no one else would see his document. Unfortunately, the memo started spreading within the company. The floodgates opened and previously silent employees started talking. To quell dissent, we: told executives to write to their employees condemning the memo; manipulated our internal Memegen to bias the ratings towards anti-Damore posts (the head of Memegen is an "ally" to the diversity cause); and gave every manager talking points on what to tell their reports about the memo. In all our communications, we concentrated on how hurt employees purportedly were and diverted attention from Google's discriminatory employment practices and political hegemony, never mind the science. We needed to make an example of Damore. [Backup .pdf on Google: https://drive.google.com/file/d/1GdND66w9zLxGzIxoY3nYk1iR-Wb3ub_kX/view.]

Trejo, Shane. "Alex Jones Goes DEFCON 5: Donald Trump Needs to 'Wake the F**k Up' on Tech Censorship." *Big League Politics*, About Big League Politics, 30 July 2019, https://bigleaguepolitics.com/alex-jones-goes-defcon-5-donald-trump-needs-to-wake-the-fk-up-on-tech-censorship/.

Conspiracy maven Alex Jones of *Infowars* sent an urgent message to President Donald Trump on Monday to "wake the f**k up" regarding tech censorship, believing it is the President's "Achilles heel" that may stop him from gaining re-election in 2020. "In just the last three days, Mr. President," Jones said in an urgent address to Trump, "we have seen over two-hundred-million followers to scores of popular Instagram and Facebook accounts deleted and the accounts removed."

Wu, Nicholas. "Tulsi Gabbard Sues Google, Claims 'Election Interference' over Suspension of Ad Account." *USA Today*, Gannett Satellite Information Network, 25 July 2019, https://www.usatoday.com/story/news/politics/elections/2019/07/25/tulsi-gabbard-democrat-candidate-sues-google/1828271001/.

On Thursday, member of Congress and Democratic presidential candidate Tulsi Gabbard launched a lawsuit against Google claiming "serious and continuing violations of Tulsi's right to free speech" because of Google's suspension of the Gabbard campaign's advertising account during the first Democratic presidential debate. The campaign asks for an immediate court injunction to stop further meddling from Google and payment of financial damages. According to the lawsuit, filed by lawyers representing Gabbard's campaign Tulsi Now Inc., Google suspended the Gabbard campaign's advertising account for several hours during the first Democratic debate, when Gabbard was briefly the most-searched candidate on Google.

# Appendix B

## Best Facebook Statuses, Year to Date
## By Michael Rectenwald

**Michael Rectenwald**
21 hrs ·
I'm fairly convinced that the loftier the abstractions a person uses, the more noble-sounding their political ideals, the greater the likelihood of their being a totalitarian. Watch out for words like "equity, diversity and inclusion," or even "the People," "the common good," "the general welfare," and "brotherhood of man." When in the mouths of politicos, these are the watchwords of totalitarianism.

**Michael Rectenwald shared a memory.**
Yesterday at 3:15 PM ·
Last year on this day I was on *Tucker Carlson Tonight* talking about the Red Guard zealots who ruined my academic career bc they are jealous zeroes & sexist-racists who couldn't write a sentence. Today I finished my 9th book. One of these zealots has published 1 essay in 20 years, and that in the rag called the *Nation*. That's what's happening to US higher education.

**Michael Rectenwald**
August 2 at 11:11 PM ·
By means of propaganda, the Communists succeeded in making people believe that their conduct had universal implications, relevant to humanity as a whole. Critics have often tried to make a distinction between Nazism and Communism by arguing that the Nazi project had a particular aim, which was nationalist and racist in the extreme, whereas Lenin's project was universal. This is entirely wrong. In both theory and practice, Lenin and his successors excluded from humanity all capitalists, the bourgeoisie, counterrevolutionaries, and others, turning them into absolute enemies in their sociological and political discourse. Kautsky noted as early as 1918 that these terms were entirely elastic, allowing those in power to exclude whomever they wanted from humanity whenever they so wished. These were the terms that led directly to crimes against humanity.

There were many examples of this process. During the great trials in Moscow, the procurator Andrei Vyshinsky, who was an intellectual with a traditional classical training, threw himself into a veritable frenzy of animalization:

"Shoot these rabid dogs! Death to this gang who hide their ferocious teeth, their eagle claws, from the people! Down with that vulture Trotsky, from whose mouth a bloody venom drips,

putrefying the great ideals of Marxism! Let's put these liars out of harm's way, these miserable pygmies who dance around rotting carcasses! Down with these abject animals! Let's put an end once and for all to these miserable hybrids of foxes and pigs, these stinking corpses! Let their horrible squeals finally come to an end! Let's exterminate the mad dogs of capitalism, who want to tear to pieces the flower of our new Soviet nation! Let's push the bestial hatred they bear our leaders back down their own throats!"
(Qtd. In *The Black Book of Communism*, p. 750.)

Michael Rectenwald
June 19 ·
I think Trump should marry Putin. Can the social justice left condemn a man for who he loves?

Michael Rectenwald
July 18 at 2:51 AM ·
If you're hearing dog whistles, maybe you're a dog.

Michael Rectenwald
June 17 ·
If the Democrats & their media proxies had a tenth of Cornell West's spirituality, they might be worth listening to. As it is, they are just a party of hate. Btw, thanks so much to you, my friends. Amazing grace.

Michael Rectenwald
July 11 at 10:48 PM ·
Stepped down to post this to AOC. Now back to book...

 **Michael Rectenwald**
@antipcnyuprof

@AOC You're an algorithmic-driven generator of plug-n-play phrases from the prescribed woke-book & premised on a cartoon history marked by myopic Manichean & stunning historical and political illiteracy. You don't have "thoughts"but rather predictable woke word vomit episodes.

10:22 PM · Jul 11, 2019 · Twitter Web Client

ılı View Tweet activity

Michael Rectenwald
July 2 ·
Train stopped in Harrisburg, where I lived the small life in nearby Carlisle, PA, serving my ex- and kissing her ass as I curtailed my true range and ability to fit into a "nice" college community where my ex- worked (and still does). I am not a good "community member," as such. I'm not a bad person either but my role is not to be a mere "good egg," as my ex was wont to refer to the acceptable people. Meanwhile not until I was long gone did I see how much trying to please others, especially her and her goody-two-shoe ilk, trammeled and squelched me, keeping me from becoming myself. As such, she fades into oblivion (as I told her she would) while I have become...at least a nuisance. I'll leave it to my friends to suggest what I have done, but by no means am I fishing for compliments. I'm whaling for them.

**Michael Rectenwald**
July 2 ·
I shared an Uber in the lower east side of Manhattan. Some unsavory blue-haired "woman" kept gratuitously clearing her throat. Then when she got out she pleasantly thanked the driver—after yelling at him for sitting seconds extra at a green light—and then once out the door turned toward me and grumbled "go fuck yourself"—making me feel very gratified. Either she recognized my (in)famous self, or saw me trying to open a *Medium* article called "Is 'cis' offensive?" I was surely about to say that it's no more offensive than dianetics but an equally fabricated and nonsensical shibboleth. But I couldn't get the stupid article open so that must not have been it. Either my invitation of Milo to speak in my class is still sticking in the labial craw of these gender elastic lunatics or else she just pegged me as "cis-heteronormative" and thus worthy of contempt like the left-behind after the genderific rapture. Whatever the case, I feel quite healthy and self-satisfied, which should help my writing while en route to Pittsburgh, where the polymorphism is not yet an epidemic.

**Michael Rectenwald**
June 29 ·
Leftists are the predestinarians—and the "predestined"—of the secular world.

**Michael Rectenwald**
June 20 ·
All the "gender trouble" (to quote Judith the Butler) began with the introduction in 1955 by John Money (that's right) of the word "gender" to refer to human sex difference. Before that, "gender" referred to language! Thanks "John Money." That's why I call it the "gender jackpot" in *Springtime for Snowflakes*.

**Michael Rectenwald**

June 13 ·

"Horkheimer and Adorno both diagnosed the rise of German fascism, Stalinist lineage, and consumer capitalism in the same light: failure of the revolutionary potency of the working class."

No, Brutus, the failure is in yourselves and your treatment of the working class as cannon fodder to settle your pathetic resentments and surreptitious and dishonest will to power. Cowards.

**Michael Rectenwald**

May 20 ·

The singularity is going to amount to an open-air prison state thanks to Chinese tracking and Silicon Valley social justice AI bots correcting us, directing us, surveilling on us, reporting us, even taking over our vehicles and taking us to places we never meant to go. You'll see it all in the *Google Archipelago* in much more detail and haunting prose. Plus you'll find out how all the elements function, fit together, coalesce—what they're all doing and to what end.

**Michael Rectenwald**

May 18 ·

Hey lefties, there is no such thing as "whiteness". "Whiteness" is an abstraction, a proxy, and a repository into which you deposit your own "white guilt," which you then place at a safe distance, so that you may disown it—or, if needed, withdraw in smaller sums as if electronically, so as to project it onto those other, unregenerate "whites" (the "real whites"?), whose "whiteness" is evil but which you, by virtue of your legerdemain, do not share.

But aren't you forgetting something—namely, that you are "white?" Yet you are somehow exempt from the evil of "whiteness." Is that because you have consciously transcended "whiteness?" In that case, you've just proven that what you've defined as determinative in some significant sense ultimately doesn't define you, and thus, by extension, anyone else.

See, your "construction of whiteness" represents a textbook example of the fallacy of reification, only in reverse. Reification is making abstractions into things. You've taken a "thing," a trait shared by a population group, and turned it into an abstraction. But then you've gone further yet; you've descended deeper into ideational error and proceeded to personify your abstraction. That would be fine in poetry (although almost unavoidably hokey and productive of extended metaphor, which rarely succeeds), but in political discourse, such category mistakes are dehumanizing—to the very people whose interests you purport to advocate. And such dreadful butcheries of thought and language amount to a bloody abortion in the public sphere. Keep your dumb ideas to yourself?

I don't blame you for your many category mistakes, however. You didn't study logic. Almost no one does now. You were told that, like science and math, logic is a tool of oppression, an element in a "master narrative" that props up white supremacy. Logic is racist.

I'd say that such a notion—which you wouldn't dare examine and haven't explicitly stated the implications of, because when you "unpack" and "deconstruct" texts, they are never your own—represents the real racism in the room. It suggests that black people must be victims of mental operations that they are incapable of performing, and that the use of such mental tools must always be wielded by others and amounts necessarily to their disadvantage. That means game over, you lose. Your hands are tied. You have no means of self-assertion or defense. The tools of the master are too powerful to overcome.

Who's the white supremacist again?

Michael Rectenwald
May 17 ·
A major part of leftist ideology is seeing oneself and one's perspective as marginalized or somehow suppressed. The definition of being a leftist includes seeing oneself as a subordinated underdog. I know; I spent at least fifteen years cultivating this disposition.

Meanwhile, there is now no question in my mind that leftism is the dominant ideology and that its dominance is due in no small part to this intrinsically defensive posturing, with all of its baying, yelping, and querulous remonstrances—with its incredible capacity for self-deception, its need and ability to imagine that it is losing when it in fact it is dominating entirely. This surely must be an evolutionary tactic of leftist political survival.

How successful is the left? Well, for one, all of its political crimes are swept under the carpet, ignored, or justified. Yes, yes, in passing, one will acknowledge the 94 million murdered by communist regimes, or the extensive programs for eugenics supported by the US left in the 20s.

But no one on the left really ever bemoans it; no one on the right ever references it while protesting; few, if any, of whatever political persuasion, do more than merely acknowledge it in passing and as if such criminality clearly had been the exception—or, presumably, due to a tacit acknowledgment of its purported noble ends, had been excused as if by divine dispensation.

Finally, an African-American activist, namely Candace Owens, is wondering aloud how and why the hideous racist eugenicist history of progressivism has never been sufficiently reckoned with. No rightwing political contingent would have gotten away with glossing over historical evidence of such genocidal aspirations—and it shouldn't and hasn't. But there goes the left, walking off Scott-free, as if its historical connections to eugenics and mass murder didn't exist. Meanwhile, leftists cannot see, they positively are forbidden to catch so much as a glimpse of the obvious proof that they are nothing like underdogs at all, but in fact, that their ideology rules.

Don't get me wrong: I am not rightwing. As a human, I believe in a wingless future. My only avowed position is as a civil, cultural, and ideally but not always practically economic libertarian.

But what I want to know is this: How does the left get away with its documented political criminality and murderous past? If being a Nazi today is rightly deemed a vile and monstrous identification, then why is it not a disgrace, why is it not abominable to call oneself a progressive or a communist? How is one instead able, not only to possess a clear conscience, but moreover to don professorial gowns with pride and grace? No other political contingent has gotten away with such a history while keeping its reputation intact; the double standard is astonishing.

I first became disturbed by the grossly differential treatment of leftist political criminality when I tried to research it. I saw the evidence of buried and ignored evidence—that academics and other scholars had expunged, scrubbed and utterly extirpated leftist political criminality from the records in their fields. And it continues to this day. Naturally, I only began to notice the history and the coverups after I had been released from the iron-curtain grip of leftist ideology.

**Michael Rectenwald**
May 15 ·
Every noble-sounding phrase causes me immediate suspicion.

## Michael Rectenwald

May 15 ·

Since leaving academia and yet still reading academic scholarship, I recognize now more than ever what utterly patent, cliché, unoriginal, derivative, ideologically homogeneous and facile shit so much of it is. And academics are, in general, not the radicals that they imagine themselves to be but rather the most pusillanimous conformists on earth.

Addendum: For clueless leftists flitting to my posts who think that I was booted from NYU, you are completely mistaken. Read the actual history, and figure it out for yourselves, with your vast powers of inference, what really happened. I was never fired from NYU. I was PROMOTED and later RETIRED under "amicable" terms, and that is all that I can say about it. Only a moronic leftist would fail to understand the meaning of this. And yet they are still flocking to my pages like the lost, filthy, shitting carrier pigeons of misinformation and fake history that they are.

## Michael Rectenwald

May 10 ·

Looking back at Facebook "memories" from ten years ago, I realize I don't remember who I was.

## Michael Rectenwald

May 7 ·

A great deal of ideological pressure is being put on millennials and younger to eschew traditional relationships and sexuality and to choose anything but marriage and family. This is all part of the agenda to destroy any unit of organization that stands between the state or powerful monopolistic corporations as the state, and the masses. There are very nefarious forces at work that are trying to destroy all of our social ontologies, that is to say everything that constitutes social organization or that has to do with social organization, including all the pieces or parts that are necessary for it.

**Michael Rectenwald**
May 7 ·
All of the "toxicity" that they're squeezing out of men will be transferred to the sexbot.

**Michael Rectenwald**
April 30 ·
The rightwing-leftwing axis means nothing to me. Are they totalitarians or not? Totalitarianism is my enemy.

**Michael Rectenwald**
April 27 ·
What's my beef with [Jordan] Peterson? Nothing. My beef is with the cultural and intellectual ignorance that has him speaking on matters regarding which he knows next to nothing.

If you were an actual expert in Marxism and postmodern theory while the views of a dilettante with reference to the topics were continuously solicited, how might you feel?

Better yet, how might Peterson feel if I were constantly called upon to discuss psychology while he was ignored? And this while both of us are known for bucking the dominant ideology and holding almost identical views regarding the latter?

**Michael Rectenwald**
April 24 ·
"Beyond Feminism for Men: Toward a New Mating Strategy for Beta Cuckolds"

**Michael Rectenwald**
April 24 ·
Sketch of Democratic Party Platform, 2020:
1. Legalized infanticide; everyone should have the right to kill babies! We want to kill babies! It's our right!
2. Full voting rights for felons; the Boston bombers have a right to choose their victims, and their representatives!
3. Free everything, including federal funding of infanticide.
4. Make everything and everyone green (with envy).
5. Elections must be decided by intersectional score keeping as part of the Oppression Olympics.
6. Kill babies!
7. No white men.
8. Actually-existing socialism for all, except for the corporate and state monopolists.
9. Kill babies!
10. Euthanasia for Bernie Sanders.


**Michael Rectenwald**
April 21 ·
Dozing off as I peer into the laptop screen, my text seems to outline the shapes of rotund leftist activists formed from paragraphs, sentences, words, and letters. Enough to scare me back awake.


**Michael Rectenwald**
April 8 ·
Let's retire the word "liberal" now. Other than classical liberals, liberals barely exist. What we have now are illiberal leftists of one stripe or another.

**Michael Rectenwald**
April 5 ·
Socialism is just an ideology used by monopolists to eliminate competition.


**Michael Rectenwald**
April 5 ·
"Socialists" are state or corporate monopolists. The former are often the unwitting dupes & puppets of the latter. @BernieSanders & @AOC are probably statists. Trotsky may have been a corporatist posing as a statist. Corporate monopolists use state monopolist ideology ("socialism") & ideologues to clear the field.


**Michael Rectenwald**
April 3 ·
It's happened. Every single Word document I've written and saved to Google Drive was put in the Google Drive trash and every single Word file is now corrupted. My life's work is gone. Google specialist says they *may be able* to restore them from a backup. But it could take 48 hours.


**Michael Rectenwald**
April 1 ·
Mill on non-conformity as value in itself:
In this age [of mediocrity], the mere example of nonconformity, the mere refusal to bend the knee to custom, is itself a service. Precisely because the tyranny of opinion is such as to make eccentricity a reproach, it is desirable, in order to break through that tyranny, that people should be eccentric. Eccentricity has always abounded when and where strength of character has abounded; and the amount of eccentricity in a society has generally been proportional to the amount of genius, mental vigor, and moral courage which it contained. That so few now dare to be eccentric marks the chief danger of the time." —J.S. Mill.

Stacey Peters is with Tina Fisk.
March 22 ·
"The only good thing is the Left eats its own. But, not fast enough." —Michael Rectenwald


Michael Rectenwald
March 16 ·
If I were a preacher, I might say to the catastrophist left: the heat you're sensing is not from global warming, it's the encroachment of hell.


Michael Rectenwald
March 14 ·
The U.S. university system has reached such a decrepit state that one cannot but have grave doubts about its worth and justification for existing.

Along with an almost, if not entirely, exclusionary identity-based favoritism in student admissions and faculty hiring (as if people were lollipops (suckers) and the university's primary mission was to represent every flavor); with college prep companies that basically undertake the entire admissions process on behalf of prospective students, from test preparation through writing admission essays; with grade inflation run utterly amok, such that "D" is at least a "B+" or more likely an "A-"; with social justice ideology pumped into students as if intravenously and usually as a replacement for curricular content, although pretended as a supplement; with the Western cultural legacy under assault, being gutted and dispensed with in favor of victimology studies; with intersectionality becoming the official measurement of moral worth and the "most subordinated" winning the trophies in the Oppression Olympics, which represents a great deal of what goes on in the academy, where the main objective is to be "more-subordinated-than thou"; with faculty encapsulated in echo chambers enclosing shibboleth-repeating drones whose product includes victimology studies, elaborate virtue signaling rituals, and identity politics propaganda, as well as students turned into robotic slogan-chanting leftist mobs; with slogans like #BlackLivesMatter repeated one hundred times qualifying as a successful admissions essay at Stanford University; with the best faculty driven out and the worst turned into deans, dean-lets, sub-deans, dean of deans; with an enormous and burgeoning glut of administrators that now includes a vast new swath of "diversity" officers whose combined salaries amount to tens of millions of dollars in most large universities and whose function is to find if not invent "micro-aggressions" and "bias infractions"; with all of this chicanery, corruption, delegitimization, hyper-politicization, indoctrination and devaluation of the degree coming at a cost that all but the scions of immense wealth will mortgage their futures to afford, one must doubt the value and in fact wonder whether this monstrosity will or even had better collapse under its own weight. And one wonders what, at this point, would be the loss, if anything.


**Michael Rectenwald**
March 7 ·
"Tone policing" gets new meaning; Will Smith "not black enough" for Williams role.


**Michael Rectenwald**
March 2 ·
Nearly every academic in the US is operating under a dogma that they cannot even see as such, or if they do see, dare not to contradict. This has restrained thinking to such an extent that the acolytes of academia are analogous to medieval monks chanting the same mantras in unison, day after day. And, the whole enterprise has produced phrase-mongering robotic loons of the left, people who imagine they are thinking when indeed they are merely repeating and reassembling plug-n-play phraseology they've imbibed during the many sessions of uni-

versity indoctrination. There are sacred cows, like identity categories that cannot be questioned but only revered and bowed down to. There are saints, those who've written the canonical social justice bible, whose contradictory and often outrageously erroneous conclusions must be accepted as the premises of future studies. There are hundreds of unexamined beliefs and nostrums that cannot be called into question, let alone contradicted. The university system is a religious body and the religionists mouth the bromides of an ill-conceived, self-contradictory, anti-empirical, anti-rational and authoritarian creed. The creed is imposed by threat of excommunication and the dungeons of isolation. They have not stopped and cannot stop me.

**Michael Rectenwald**
February 27 ·
Socialism has been a ruling-class production all along. That's a fact, not a theory.

**Michael Rectenwald**
February 16 ·
Could this be so: leftism is to the political what entropy is to the natural realm?

**Michael Rectenwald**
February 12 ·
Just when I thought our culture had reached the nadir, it gets worse. It's as if history is running downhill.

**Michael Rectenwald**
February 7 ·
Leftist thinking as algorithmic:
The left is all about the ends justifying the means, even if the means utterly contradict the desired ends. The left is charac-

terized by a deterministic algorithmic "thinking"—if A, that is, if A is the desired object, then, these are the necessary steps to obtain A, including, if necessary, not-A. The ends utterly determine the means, including the commission of acts that are antithetical, morally and politically, to the ends sought.

Thus, shortly after a revolution undertaken putatively on behalf of the working class for their control of society, Lenin ordered the first post-revolutionary striking government workers shot dead, and the murders were committed without hesitation.

**Michael Rectenwald**
February 3 ·
This post is not about the Super Bowl, not even the weird beer ad with the alienated robot who outperforms everyone in every area but is left on the outside looking in when the people drink beer and socialize—some sort of compensation thrown to the many about to be made redundant by AI, I suppose. Otherwise, what a boring game for a sport that sells itself with high scoring.

But I wanted to write about how the leftist agenda is now fully compatible with the global corporate agenda. Even the NFL is a social justice league. Sounds wonderful, right? Strange how leftism is now the dominant ideology yet leftists still imagine that they are radicals. How they don't see that their politics, first produced in the academy, has been absorbed by social media, mass media, corporate America, and now even the NFL.

Kirk Meighoo writes, "The left have entered a weird, contradictory alliance with the largest corporations in the world to push a globalist agenda." I'm glad that I'm not alone in seeing this, but I am studying the extent to which it is really new. Marx and Engels were globalists and hoped for the dissolution of all nations and differences by global capitalism, at which point global socialism would be possible. What's new though is the explicit adoption of leftism by the world's largest corporations for the purposes of global governmentalism and global corporatism.

Michael Rectenwald

January 19 ·

Once you really get the gist of it, academic writing, or writing for academic journals, periodicals and book publishers, is much easier than popular writing, or writing for broader, popular audiences.

Now I'm going to tell you why that is.

When writing academic prose, if/when one is not perfectly sure about what one is saying and thus does not express it in a perfectly clear way, one can often get away with it. In fact, one can even can *use* obscurantism to make any argument less than clear, or even impenetrable or utterly unintelligible—on purpose!

How is that, you ask? As with any writing, but especially in academic writing, the reader may assume that an idea is coherent but that they, the reader, simply does not understand it. The obscurity is written off to the difficulty of the idea itself, rather than to the writer's failure to clearly express the idea. This works much more often in academic writing but not so much in popular writing, for reasons explained below. Hint: it's not because academic ideas are necessarily so intrinsically difficult that their clear expression is nearly impossible.

In academic writing, despite or even because of difficulty, the reader is compelled to keep reading, because they need to know what the writer is saying, especially if the writing is published by a reputable source—but sometimes even when it is not. The reader of academic writing is not reading strictly (or even at all) for pleasure, personal gratification, or even to gain some important understanding or enlightenment. The academic reader must remain *au courant* in the field. The reader is reading primarily to gain something they can *trade* in the academic marketplace, as it were. Academia operates as a *gift economy*, under which one makes contributions to a field, not usually (or even at all) for money, but rather for recognition that one *trades* for other goods, like jobs, grants, tenure, etc. One also reads for the same reason—not primarily for the intrinsic value of the reading, but rather for the cultural capital one can gain and then trade—either as part of one's own writing, for a job, for career advancement, and so on.

The reader of popular writing has a wholly different relationship to the text. Generally. they are reading for the intrinsic value of the experience. They are reading to experience pleasure, receive entertainment, find distraction from less pleasant thoughts, gain knowledge, or seek enlightenment of one kind or another, and so on. So, present this reader with obscurity and that obscurity better damn well be a function of the difficulty of the idea itself, or else you will lose the reader. And you may lose the reader anyway. The point is that the popular reader is usually under no professional *obligation*, special duty, or other extrinsic compulsion to read anyone's writing, and no academic is an exception until they become relevant outside of the strict confines of the discipline. Therefore, to keep that reader reading (the object of all writing), or to capture that reader in the first place, the writing should be clear, compelling, and the reading of it should represent a pleasurable experience in itself. The popular reader has no real marketplace where they can trade your contribution, so one can't count on their patience or dutiful continuance at all.

Why am I writing this? Because I'm now working on my second popular book and realizing how much more difficult such writing is than writing academic prose.

**Michael Rectenwald**
January 15 ·

Being a good leftist involves the rehearsal of a set of scripts, replete with a standardized vocabulary and a thrifty method for handily categorizing, sorting, and finally dispensing with whole areas of existence by means of political algorithms as such. Leftism is formulaic and involves the shortcutting of thinking. Ready-made answers to expected questions are distributed to loosely-affiliated "members" on a regular basis through formal and informal discourses, including academic and "political" discursive means. Leftism is a tight, neat package for living and also a straight-jacket—for those who demand too much freedom of motion, that is.

**Michael Rectenwald**
January 15 ·
If Gillette really believed in toxic masculinity, they wouldn't berate men about it while selling them razor blades.

**Michael Rectenwald**
January 7 ·
So much contemporary social science and humanities "scholarship" consists of nothing more than thinly-veiled political propaganda, and/or elaborate virtue-signaling rituals.

**Michael Rectenwald**
January 2 ·
The echo chamber of the humanities and social sciences in academia is almost hermetically sealed. One never encounters real divergence or actually singular and independent minds. It takes a crisis to crack this iron cage. One might look at the typical academic leftist as a hostage. That's how I remained a communist for so long. The boneyard was well hidden.

# Index

209

214

CPSIA information can be obtained
at www.ICGtesting.com
Printed in the USA
LVHW030749090919
630389LV00003B/62

9 781943 003266